Pass the Praxis II® Test

Principles of Learning and Teaching

Third Edition

Christina Shorall

Carlow University

Boston, Massachusetts
Columbus, Ohio

8 9 10 11 12 V0CR 15 14 13 12
ISBN-13: 978-0-13-714912-4
ISBN-10:   0-13-714912-3

DEDICATION

Marca Paparozzi

Role model and businesswoman extraordinaire

CONTENTS

CHAPTER 2

THE COGNITIVE DEVELOPMENT OF STUDENTS

A review of how your students will develop cognitively encompasses assessing their capabilities at various stages. The subject of cognitive development in the *Principles of Learning and Teaching* exam requires you to display a working knowledge of four facets of development:

- Cognitive Ability
- Social and Cultural Aspects of Cognitive Development
- Information Processing
- Linguistic Development

Cognitive Ability

Jean Piaget proposed the most comprehensive theory of cognitive ability. Piaget's four **stages of development** provide teachers with a framework for the cognitive characteristics of certain ages and the accompanying educational implications. Piaget's theory emphasizes the importance of active participation and reminds teachers that students think differently at different stages of their lives. Piaget believed that while all people pass through the four stages, they might proceed at different rates.

Schemes, according to Piaget, are an individual's generalized way of responding to the world. These schemes are methods of organization. New information is adapted into existing schemes by processes referred to as assimilation, accommodation and equilibration. *Assimilation* occurs when people deal with a new experience in a manner that is consistent with a present scheme. *Accommodation* occurs when people must incorporate a new experience that requires them to modify an old scheme or form a new scheme. *Equilibration*, a period of flux, happens when individuals are attempting to adjust prior schemes with new experiences that do not fit into their existing schemes. Examples of these three concepts are:

- *Assimilation:* a five-year-old identifies a clog as a type of shoe
- *Accommodation:* the five-year-old recognizes the clog is made of glass and cannot be an actual shoe

- *Equilibration:* the period of time when the five-year-old must mentally wrestle with the clog dilemma until he or she can explain the object in terms of an existing or new schema: A clog can be either a shoe or a decoration

By understanding the approximate ages, characteristics, and educational implications of cognitive development stages, teachers can identify children with developmental delays or talents and select or design age appropriate activities.

Sensorimotor (ages 0–2).

Characteristics:

- Cognitive development comes through use of body and senses
- No object permanence until later in this stage
- Language absent until end of period
- Egocentrism

Educational implications:

- Provide multiple objects for stimulation of various shapes, colors, and sizes
- Allow students to actively engage environmental objects

Preoperational (ages 2–7).

Characteristics:
- Begins using symbols but cannot manipulate them
- Realism, animism, artificialism, transductive reasoning, centering, egocentrism and irreversibility
- Beginnings of representation
- Egocentric and socialized speech

Educational Implications:

- Deferred imitation, symbolic play, drawing, and mental images
- Encourage the use of language

Concrete operations (ages 7–11).

Characteristics:

- Can perform mental operations with the use of concrete objects, not verbal statements
- Conservation, seriation, classification and number concepts
- Verbal understanding

Educational implications:

- Classification activities
- Integrated activities that allow students to make connections between ideas previously thought to be separate

Formal operations (age 11 and up).

Characteristics:

- Released from the restrictions of tangible and concrete
- May separate real from the possible, hypothetic/deductive reasoning
- Development of logico-mathematical structures
- Language freed from concrete, able to express the possible

Educational implications:

- Challenge, do not frustrate
- Be aware of adolescent limitations
- Encourage analysis of information in drawing conclusions

Social and Cultural Aspects of Cognitive Development

The social and cultural environments of your students affect their cognitive development. Lev Vygotsky proposed that children's social interactions with those more knowledgeable could actually aid in cognitive development. Vygotsky's theory of a *zone of proximal development* implies an optimal time for students to learn. In this zone students with assistance from more knowledgeable others can grasp ideas that they would otherwise not be able to attain. It is the span between unactualized potential to actualized potential.

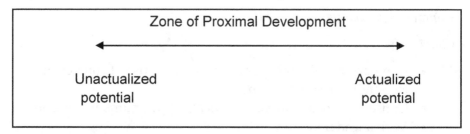

Figure 2.1 Zone of Proximal Development

Jerome Bruner used the word *scaffolding* for the support learners need to receive when faced with a task that presents too much of a challenge to accomplish alone. The support students receive in the zone of proximal development can be referred to as scaffolding:

- An actual development level exists (capabilities without help)
- A level of potential development exists (capabilities with assistance)
- The zone of proximal development equals the area of potential development an individual is capable of attaining with assistance from a more competent partner (teacher/student/parent)

The social aspect of Vygotsky's theory hinges on the interaction between learners and mentors (or students and teachers) in the zone of proximal development. Methods exist to maximize effectiveness:

- Relating new knowledge to prior knowledge assists in understanding
- Tasks should be designed from less to more complex as the student becomes increasingly sophisticated
- Apprenticeship consists of working with an expert, thinking and planning how to perform a task
- Interaction with peers helps by having similar others explain concepts and justify ideas

Information Processing

Information processing theory emphasizes the impact of maturity on cognition. As students grow, their attention, learning strategies, knowledge base, and metacognitive ability improves. Information processing theory emphasizes the maturation of cognitive processes.

Attention:

- As children grow, they become less easily distracted
- Children learn what they *intend* to learn

Learning strategies:

- As children grow, they use rehearsal strategies
- As children grow, organization improves
- As children grow, learning strategies become increasingly efficient
- Elaboration emerges around puberty

Knowledge base:

- As children grow, their amount of knowledge increases
- As children grow, their knowledge base becomes increasingly integrated
- The more information children have, the easier it is to remember things

Metacognition:

- As children grow, knowledge of their own cognitive processes improves
- As children grow, they become more aware of their limitations
- As children grow, they become more aware of effective learning strategies

A simple rule for designing the length of activities equates with age. According to conventional wisdom, the age of the child is a guide to the number of minutes she can attend to any given task. A ten-year-old student can pay attention for ten minutes.

Linguistic Development

Language development encompasses sound, structure, meaning, and context. Most of our language acquisition is complete by the age of four or five. For this reason, young children should be encouraged and given opportunities to talk. All children in all cultures progress at the same rate linguistically under normal circumstances.

The Components of Language:

- *Phonemes:* the smallest unit of sound
- *Morphemes:* the smallest unit with meaning (like a base or an affix, for example *ed*)
- *Semantics:* the meaning
- *Syntax:* the sentence structure
- *Pragmatics:* the use of language to communicate
- *Phonology:* the sound system of language

The Development of Language:

- Cooing: 6–8 weeks
- Babbling: approximately 4 months
- Holophrasic: approximately 1 year
- Single words, multiple meanings: about 18 months
- Experiences with tense and number: 18 months and older
- Simple sentences: about 2 years

Common irregularities.

Young children occasionally make errors in their use of language, with the most common types of errors being overgeneralization, undergeneralization and overregularization.

- *Overgeneralization:* overextending the use of a word by using one label for several objects (using the word *dog* for a cow or horse)
- *Undergeneralization:* being too restrictive in the application of a word by leaving out situations when the word applies (applying the word *animal* only to those animals with fur)
- *Overregularization:* incorrectly applied grammar (using the past tense *ed* as in *she comed*)

CHAPTER 3

THE PSYCHOSOCIAL DEVELOPMENT OF STUDENTS

As a teacher, how will you structure your classroom to maximize positive psychosocial development? Teachers must consider the factors effecting students' psychosocial development as well as cognitive development. Self-image, social interaction, moral reasoning—all facets of psychosocial development—can contribute to academic success. The *Principles of Learning and Teaching* exam contains questions relating to several psychosocial topics:

- Social Interaction
- Adolescent Development
- Patterns of Moral Growth
- Parenting Styles and Their Impact
- Contemporary Issues Affecting Social Development
- Self-Esteem
- Self-Control

Social Interaction

Erik Erikson proposed that eight *stages of psychosocial development* exist spanning from birth through adulthood. Each stage contains a development crisis. Each crisis stage has the potential for a positive or a negative outcome. Positive experiences lead to positive outcomes and negative experiences lead to negative outcomes. While Erikson suggests a range of ages for each stage, variations occur.

General education teachers must consider stages one through five of Erik Erikson's eight stages. The five stages are explained in terms of the age, the positive social experiences, the negative social experiences and the educational implications.

Stage 1: Trust vs. mistrust (age 0–18 months).
- *Trust:* If nurtured and basic needs are met, children learn that others can be dependable and reliable.
- *Mistrust:* If there is cold parental care or lack of nurturing, children learn the world is undependable, unpredictable and possibly dangerous.

- *Educational implications:* Meet physical needs consistently and provide physical affection at regular intervals.

Stage 2: Autonomy vs. shame (age 18 months–3 years).

- *Autonomy:* If self-sufficient behavior is encouraged in appropriate venues, children develop as individuals.
- *Shame:* If caretakers demand too much and no autonomy is allowed, children develop shame and doubt about their ability to handle problems.
- *Educational implications:* Provide consistent, reasonable discipline, opportunities for students to do for themselves, and positive role models.

Stage 3 :Initiative vs. guilt (ages 3–6).

- *Initiative:* If independence to plan and undertake activities is given, children learn to plan and take responsibility for their own needs and activities.
- *Guilt:* If adults discourage a child's plans or activities, children develop guilt about needs and desires.
- *Educational implications:* Support efforts to plan and carry out activities, help with realistic choices that consider others needs.

Stage 4: Industry vs. inferiority (ages 6–12—a critical period for building self-esteem).

- *Industry:* If patterns of working hard, persisting at lengthy tasks and putting work before pleasure are rewarded, children learn to take pride in their accomplishments.
- *Inferiority:* If children are punished or cannot meet expectations, feelings of inferiority about their own abilities develop.
- *Educational implications:* Provide opportunities for children to achieve recognition and praise by producing things.

Stage 5: Identity vs. role confusion (ages 12–18 — a critical period for building self-esteem).

- *Identity:* If students are treated as adults and challenged with realistic goals, they will achieve a sense of identity regarding the role they will play as adults.
- *Role confusion:* If students are treated as children, they may have mixed ideas and feelings about where they fit in society.
- *Educational implications:* Treat students as adults, challenge them with realistic goals, and address issues of identity.

Adolescent Development

As you might recall from your own adolescence, the social and emotional issues experienced during this time eclipse academic concerns. Adolescence spans approximately ages 12 through 18, with boys maturing later than girls. The role of peer influence is critical. Students typically believe they are the center of everyone's attention, a behavior referred to as the **imaginary audience**. The belief of teenagers that they are completely unlike anyone else is referred to as a **personal fable**. James Marcia proposed four responses that adolescents exhibit when they need to make choices that affect their identity.

- *Identity diffusion:* inability to commit to choices
- *Identity foreclosure:* making a commitment based on someone else's choices
- *Identity moratorium:* desire to make a choice, but not now
- *Identity achievement:* committing to choices and consistently maintaining them

As a teacher, you will want to consider the identity status of your individual students. By providing opportunities to explore belief systems and career options within a social context, students will begin to develop a sense of self. Freedom from indecision allows students more time to concentrate on academic pursuits.

Patterns of Moral Growth

Moral reasoning also appears to have developmental stages. In the initial stage, from birth to age two or three, children learn from their parents and through modeling. In early childhood, from two to six years of age, they learn from other authority figures in their environment. By middle childhood, six to eleven years old, students learn from making and following rules and derive insight into morality by observing children who do not follow the rules. For this reason, consistency by those creating and enforcing rules is critical at this stage. By adolescence, approximately twelve to eighteen years of age, teens learn to control impulsivity that clashes with rules. Adults become firmer with adolescents. Students look to their peers for acceptance and incorporate them into their decision-making process.

Lawrence Kohlberg proposed three *levels of moral reasoning,* each containing two stages.

Level I: Preconventional morality (ages 4–10).

- *Punishment-avoidance:* Obedience is based solely on the individual. Students will disobey if they can avoid being caught.
- *Exchange of favors:* Right and wrong are defined in terms of consequences to the individual. Children recognize others have needs, too.

Level II: Conventional morality (ages 10–13).

- *Good boy/good girl:* Moral decisions are based upon what actions please others. Intentions are important.
- *Law and order:* Children perceive rules to be inflexible and it is their duty to obey them.

Level III: Postconventional morality.

- *Social contract:* Rules represent agreement among many people. Rules are considered flexible and can be changed if inadequate.
- *Universal ethical principle:* Individual's universal principles transcend concrete rules. People follow their inner conscience.

Educational implications for patterns of moral development.

The following suggestions will enhance moral development and facilitate moral behavior in your classroom:

- Establish a firm, yet supportive, authoritative environment.
- Help students recognize how their actions affect others.

- Provide students with practice in recognizing others' emotional states.
- Display and reward models of moral and pro-social behavior.
- Discuss moral issues and dilemmas as they arise, daily and in the curriculum.

Parenting Styles and Their Impact

Parents and teachers have the greatest impact on children. As a teacher you must be aware of how parenting styles affect the psychosocial development of students. Four major styles exist. For each style the following are included: what the parent *provides*, who is *created* by that style of parenting, and the appropriate *teacher response*.

*The **Authoritative** Parent:*

- *Provides:* love, support, and consistency with rules
- *Creates:* self-confident, independent, and respectful child
- *Teacher response:* adopt authoritative style

*The **Authoritarian** Parent:*

- *Provides:* little warmth, high expectation, and little regard for child's opinions or needs
- *Creates:* anxious, low self-confidence, and coercive child
- *Teacher response:* adopt authoritative style, provide warmth, and solicit perspectives

*The **Permissive** Parent:*

- *Provides:* love, few expectations, and no consequences
- *Creates:* selfish, dependent, and impulsive child
- *Teacher response:* adopt authoritative style, high expectations, and consequences

*The **Uninvolved** Parent:*

- *Provides:* no emotional support, few expectations, and little interest in child
- *Creates:* low self-control, absence of long-term goals, and disobedient child
- *Teacher response:* adopt authoritative style, emotional warmth, high expectations, and consequences

15

Contemporary Issues Affecting Social Development

While all of your students will experience social dilemmas, some will face situations or crises that affect classroom performance. These behaviors range from simply impacting student interaction to placing students at risk of dropping out of school. Teachers who understand the psychosocial consequences of situations or crises such as day care, divorce, homelessness, poverty, and abuse are better equipped to identify and assist their students in finding solutions.

Day Care:

- Best staffed by teachers who specialize in day-care services
- Good day care advances cognitive and language development
- Children are more assertive, independent, and self-confident
- Children are less pleasant, polite, and compliant

Divorce:

- More absences and disruptions
- Deterioration in peer relationships, social behavior, and academic competence

Homelessness:

- Higher rate of health problems
- Developmental delays, hunger, and poor nutrition
- Depression, anxiety, and behavioral problems
- Parental stress contributes to poor parenting and the possibility of violence
- Educational underachievement
- Teachers should assist in finding some type of stability

Poverty

- More apt to drop out of school
- Increased occurrence of pregnancy out of wedlock
- Greater exposure to health risks

Abuse:

- Underdeveloped physically
- Poor hygiene
- Developmental lags

- Injuries or improper care when injured
- Inappropriate attire
- Fear of adults
- A desire to remain at school
- Poor school attendance
- Inappropriate sexual behavior for age
- Running away from home

It is critical that you be aware of the laws that govern the reporting of child abuse in your state. Virtually every state in the nation mandates the reporting of suspected child abuse by educators. To decrease the incidence of child abuse, teachers must be alert, understanding, observant, discreet, and effective in their documentation of suspected abuse.

Self-Esteem

A strong relationship exists between social interaction and self-esteem. The messages your students receive from others in the environment guide and shape their future behavior and self-concept. Teachers influence this process by creating opportunities for success academically and socially. This requires that teachers provide students with the tools for success.

Academic tools for enhancing self-esteem.

To enhance self-esteem academically, research suggests the following strategies:

- Have high expectations, complete with support and encouragement.
- Access students' prior knowledge to ensure they have an adequate foundation.
- Design assignments to take a student step by step so errors can be identified as they occur.
- Let students know that errors give rise to better understanding, if explored.
- Give students opportunities to revise and improve their work.

Social tools for enhancing self-esteem.

To enhance self-esteem socially, research supports the following strategies:

- Establish the rules for behavior at the beginning of the year
- Be consistent and fair with all students
- Seek opportunities to praise students
- Admonish students privately
- Provide students with alternatives to undesirable behavior
- Design opportunities for positive student interaction
- Highlight talents of individual students to establish their value in the classroom

Self-Control

The concept of self-control relates to behavioral issues in the classroom. The ability to control impulses allows students to follow through with activities, control anger, and channel frustration. Reflective students—as opposed to impulsive students—achieve at higher rates, have higher emotional security, and are generally more popular.

When should you begin to look for signs of impulsivity or self-control problems? Impulsivity at four years old often leads to a troubled adolescence, according to research. By the first grade children become capable of devising strategies for self-control. By the fifth grade, if students exhibit negative playground behavior, receive low marks from their teachers regarding their social skills, or already have behavioral contracts with school administration, behavioral intervention techniques should be designed.

What are the educational implications? The sooner students receive intervention regarding negative behaviors, the better. The longer the undesirable behavior is allowed to continue, the more difficult it becomes to change the pattern.

CHAPTER 4

STUDENT DIVERSITY

By the year 2020, half of all elementary school students in America will belong to nonwhite groups. The minority will become the majority. Because of these changing demographics, teachers must be prepared to assist culturally diverse students to ensure their academic and social success.

Multicultural education refers to educational methods and curricula that respect students' unique cultures and languages. The goal of multicultural education is to provide all children with equality of opportunity. How will you teach your culturally diverse students aspects of American culture such as language and simultaneously uphold the preciousness of their native culture? The first step in understanding diversity is to acknowledge the issues surrounding multicultural education:

- Current Trends
- Goals
- Language Programs
- Instructional Adaptations
- Additional Types of Diversity

Current Trends

Current approaches to multicultural education subscribe to the belief that all ethnic groups in America contribute to society. The belief that diverse groups of people contribute their unique experiences and traditions to society as a whole is referred to as *cultural pluralism*. It follows that, in the classroom, teachers improve society by increasing cultural awareness. Banks and Banks, leaders in multicultural research, define multicultural education in the following manner:

- All students, regardless of ethnicity, should experience equal opportunities in school.
- An attempt is made to reform past invasive or oppressive practices and create equity.
- There is a continual process of designing and implementing the modifications required.

These changes in the education of ethnic students are highly controversial. Should students be taught in their own language? Should they be forced to learn English before they advance in their academics? How do the changes regarding equity for diverse students impact other groups? Does acceptance of certain diverse groups sanction or encourage alternative lifestyles?

Multicultural education became paramount when research revealed that students with limited English skills were at risk of failing academically. The dropout rate for Latino students is double that of white students. Because of the changing demographics in American schools, instructional design and delivery must be adjusted to accommodate and ensure success for all students.

Goals

Banks and Banks suggest that, in addition to adjusting instructional design and delivery, the attitudes of teachers and administrators also need to change. Some fundamental misconceptions concerning diverse populations must be addressed. It is important to keep in mind that:

- Diversity does occur within ethnic groups. It is important to recognize individual members of diverse groups as unique individuals.
- The practices of the dominant culture should not be used as models to which ethnic groups are encouraged to aspire.

By sensitizing classroom teachers, the following goals are accomplished:

- Multiple perspectives regarding information are explored creating culturally literate students.
- Students become more tolerant when they understand the connection between culture and beliefs.
- By creating an environment of acceptance, students gain the confidence to pursue opportunities previously thought unattainable.

By incorporating the traditions, beliefs and values of many cultures into the classroom, one can validate the importance of diversity in society. You can accomplish this in several ways:

- Create culturally diverse cooperative learning groups to encourage understanding and multiple perspectives.
- Incorporate the perspectives and achievements of culturally diverse individuals into the curriculum.
- Motivate culturally diverse students by drawing upon their unique experiences.
- Become familiar with the various cultures represented in your classroom to increase your understanding and appreciation for their diversity.
- Encourage the families or guardians of your students to become involved in the education of their children by attending school functions and participating in classroom activities.

Language Programs

Functioning easily in American society requires knowledge of the English language. Various methods of teaching English are used with non-English speaking students. Three basic types of English immersion programs exist.

Structured immersion:

- Used in the elementary grades
- All lessons are in the immersion language

Sheltered immersion:

- Used in secondary grades
- Subjects are taught in English
- Simple vocabulary is used

Pull-out immersion:

- Used when the diverse population is too small to merit an entire class
- Students are taken from general education classes for special instruction

Instructional Adaptations

Instructional adaptations to assist culturally diverse students exhibit similarities to some special education techniques. Individualized education programs frequently work best. Ability grouping, accommodating learning styles, programmed instruction, or computer-based programs are several ways that teachers meet the needs of students.

Ability grouping.

Ability grouping is also referred to as tracking. In the past, tracking was typically based on intelligence. Tracking based upon race, intelligence, or social class is unacceptable in most school systems today. Tracking is acceptable today if it is based upon grouping students according to interests or vocational aspirations. This type of tracking meets the goals of multicultural education. By using peer interaction coupled with proper motivation, this type of grouping can meet both educational needs and students' personal needs for affiliation.

Accommodating learning styles.

By assessing students' strengths and preferences, teachers can accommodate their unique learning styles. Do your students prefer visual, auditory, or experiential types of stimulation? Have they shown an affinity for one of Gardner's intelligences? Students blossom when teachers tap their talents and build on the subsequent success. When initial experiences are positive, students will be motivated to continue.

Programmed instruction.

Programmed instruction is sequenced instruction that takes a step-by-step approach. B. F. Skinner believed that by having students advance incrementally, respond frequently, and receive immediate feedback, they could proceed at their own pace. Programmed material that is less linear also exists. These branching programs allow students to select from alternatives as they progress through material providing an assortment of options.

Computer-based programs.

Computer use in the classroom to facilitate individualized instruction is similar to programmed instruction. The computer can present instructional sequences and, like programmed instruction, computer based programs can be matched to individual learning preferences or styles. Optimal use of computers requires teachers to specifically plan and implement objectives just as they would in the general classroom.

Additional Types of Diversity

While cultural and ethnic diversity are in the forefront of education today, you must consider three other important types of diversity to perform well on the *Principles of Learning and Teaching*. These three additional types of diversity and proper teacher responses are listed below.

- *Gender:* create equal opportunities
- *Sexual orientation:* create an atmosphere of acceptance
- *Ability:* differentiate instruction

CHAPTER 5

COGNITION AND KNOWLEDGE CONSTRUCTION

Cognitive psychology addresses such phenomena as attention, memory, concept learning, problem solving, and reasoning. Cognitive psychologists and constructivists believe that learning involves constructing individual knowledge from individual experiences. These currently popular views have influenced classroom practices in many ways. An overview of the following issues related to cognition and knowledge construction will assist you in answering questions on the *Principles of Learning and Teaching* exam:

- Basic Assumptions of Knowledge Construction
- The Human Memory
- Concept Learning
- Promoting Effective Knowledge Construction

Basic Assumptions of Knowledge Construction

For the classroom teacher, understanding the basic tenets of knowledge construction is important. Instruction should be student centered, involve problem solving, and require students to interact socially and environmentally. Additionally, the learner should be recognized as having prior knowledge, given the opportunity to interpret and elaborate, and encouraged to view errors as opportunities to learn.

Student-centered instruction.

If students participate in actual activities, the likelihood of transfer of learning to real life improves. For this reason, instruction should center on students having the experiences as opposed to the teacher merely imparting experiences. If students have the experience, they can construct an understanding that connects with their prior knowledge. Retention and recall are improved by building knowledge in this manner.

Problem solving.

Problem solving occurs when students construct concepts and apply them to problematic situations by either going beyond given information or developing their own ideas. The more closely the situation represents the world outside the classroom, the more likely students will shift their ability to other problem-solving situations. Retention, understanding, and active use of what was learned in problem solving situations is necessary to function successfully in today's world.

Interaction socially and environmentally.

Effective knowledge construction is enhanced through the social negotiation of understanding and meaning. Can your students work collaboratively? Can they define and defend their positions? By providing opportunities for students to share their views and understand the views of others, understanding and tolerance are increased.

Interaction with the environment implies that students should do some of their learning in the authentic, or actual, environment where that discipline is practiced in real life. A biology student should spend time in a lab. Students practicing their writing skills should attempt to publish or present their ideas to a wider audience.

The learner is recognized as having prior knowledge.

Because prior knowledge and misconceptions play a part in knowledge construction, teachers must assess their individual students' beliefs before instruction begins. Prior knowledge must be considered in the classroom because students will not arrive as blank slates. Students come to school with prior knowledge and concepts that influence how future learning is assimilated. Students with misconceptions will continue to misconstruct knowledge until their teachers correct them. Assessing prior knowledge accomplishes the following objectives:

- Identifies students' misconceptions that need correcting
- Determines the current level of students' understanding
- Establishes what students thought was important enough to remember
- Ascertains what students found interesting enough to remember

Interpretation and elaboration.

Active learners are more likely to construct knowledge than *passive learners.* Rather than having students merely memorize a bank of facts, teachers should require students to go beyond the information learned. Students can interpret newly learned material or elaborate on it by forming additional associations with prior knowledge or additional new knowledge.

Errors are opportunities.

Errors are defined as having an incorrect understanding or perceiving wrongly. In the traditional classroom, errors lead to low scores and consequently low self-esteem. Today, in an atmosphere that encourages process-oriented projects and performance assessment, errors can become opportunities. Teachers can require students to explain their methods and analyze why a certain pathway was unsuccessful. The process of correction leads students to explore and ultimately correct misconceptions. Because you can never be sure if misunderstandings are the fault of the student or the teacher, teachers owe it to their students to give them opportunities to improve.

The Human Memory

The model of the human memory has three major components according to many cognitive psychologists: the *sensory register*, the *working memory* (or short-term memory) and *long-term memory*. This model refers to human memory and not parts of the actual human brain.

The sensory register:
- Keeps incoming stimuli in its original structure
- Limited capacity: one second for visual images and three seconds for auditory stimulation
- When students pay attention, the information goes to the working memory
- Methods of increasing attention:
  - Put classroom information to use quickly
  - Encourage students to take notes
  - Create a stimulating environment

- Model enthusiasm
- Decrease distractions in the classroom

Working memory:

- Keeps information while it is mentally processed
- Limited capacity: five to twenty seconds
- Thinking occurs in this stage
- The information is then either stored in long-term memory or lost

Long-term memory:

- Information could be held indefinitely
- Limitless capacity
- The more information stored, the easier it is to remember new information

Assisting students with long-term memory storage.

Several methods exist to help students in their acquisition of fact-based information (**declarative knowledge**).

- *Rehearsal:* repeating the new information frequently
- *Meaningful learning:* creating an association between new and existing information
- *Organization:* drawing attention to the connections between new information
- *Elaboration:* adjoining additional information to new knowledge
- *Visual imagery:* creating a mental picture of new information
- *Mnemonics:* using patterns, acronyms, or rhymes

To assist students with their understanding and retention of **procedural knowledge**, or knowledge of how to perform in a certain manner, the following methods are suggested:

- Give a demonstration
- Present pictures
- Supply verbal feedback
- Encourage verbal rehearsal
- Make scaffolding available

Once students have acquired information, how will you ensure they can retrieve it? To minimize memory loss, you can employ four simple strategies:

- Frequently review to encourage automaticity (rapid automatic responses)
- Drill and practice
- Solicit and provide retrieval cues
- Link prior knowledge to new information

When questioning students during reviews, you should give ample time for responses. Typically teachers wait only a few seconds for students to answer a question. By increasing wait time, students' participation, quality of response, and class performance increases. Wait time also impacts teacher performance. Teachers ask a larger number of complex questions, accommodate students' interests, and exhibit higher expectations.

Concept Learning

Concepts are mental constructs of object groupings, actions, or ideas. Individuals use concepts to simplify their world. The following items are associated with the development of concepts as they relate to education:

- *Positive instances:* examples of the concept
- *Negative instances:* nonexamples of the concept
- *Defining features:* qualities present in all cases of the concept
- *Correlational features:* features that may occur but are not essential to the concept
- *Prototypes:* typical or frequently occurring examples of the concept
- *Exemplars:* display of the variety within a concept

Students might also organize their understanding by **schemas**, **scripts,** and **personal theories**. Schemas are organized bodies of information concerning specific subject matter. Scripts occur when a schema contains a predictable order of events. Personal theories are an individual's basic belief system concerning how the world functions.

Promoting Effective Knowledge Construction
Knowledge construction in the classroom can effectively be implemented through the curriculum. By infusing your curriculum with the following six concepts, you can facilitate knowledge construction. The concept, definition, and reasoning are provided.

Provide core knowledge:

- Teachers introduce the necessary subject matter to initially provide a foundation.
- Core knowledge information should be well organized, skill based, and literal.

Integrate the curriculum:

- Students use language and methodology from several disciplines to examine problems.
- Integration maintains the complexity of the actual environment.

The curriculum is open-ended:

- The scope of what might be relevant to the curriculum should not be limited.
- Students are encouraged to bring fresh perspectives and data to the existing curriculum.

Understanding multiple perspectives:

- Plausible interpretations are constructed through communication.
- Students should understand various perspectives and adopt the most relevant and useful perspective for a particular scenario.

Cognitive flexibility:

- The identification and assessment of skills are judged by flexible application, not rote memorization.
- Students should be provided with multiple examples and revisit material in different contexts.

Apprenticeship:

- Students bridge the gap between school learning and out-of-school learning by working with a mentor from the field.
- Mentors assist students in constructing plans to meet the evolving demands and circumstances of a situation.

Authentic application:

- Students apply new knowledge in a real world setting.
- Application of knowledge in an authentic setting increases the likelihood of transfer.

CHAPTER 6

CREATING AN ENVIRONMENT FOR STUDENT LEARNING

Creating an environment that leads to time on task is a function of teacher expectations and practices. Research indicates that the amount of time students spend on instruction in the classroom directly impacts achievement scores. Classroom management consisting of rules and routines must be in place in order for you to maximize instructional time and increase achievement for your students. The following topics relate to creating environments conducive to learning:

- Behaviorism
- Models of Classroom Management
- Current Trends in Classroom Management

Behaviorism

Behaviorism is a term for the theories of learning associated with observable elements of behavior. The behavioral approach in schools is often used with young students, those who have a limited capacity to learn, or students with control problems. By changing environmental conditions, behaviorists can control the behavior of students.

Classical conditioning.

Ivan Pavlov was one of the first behaviorists. *Classical conditioning* was his contribution to the field. In classical conditioning, you can program one stimulus to take over for another.

- *Unconditioned stimulus*: The teacher blows a whistle in the classroom.
- *Unconditioned response*: The students cover their ears and subsequently stop talking.
- Couple the teacher's raised hand (a conditioned stimulus) with using the whistle for a period of time and eventually the students will cover their ears and stop talking (conditioned response) with only the teacher's raised hand.

Pavlov's research contributed several terms to the world of education. Three major concepts and examples are listed:

- *Stimulus generalization:* Because children feel secure when they see a police officer's uniform, they generalize that all uniforms should make them feel safe
- *Discrimination:* The children realize that not all uniformed people are like police officers
- *Extinction:* The raised hand of the teacher no longer quiets the children

Operant conditioning.

Operant conditioning was B.F. Skinner's explanation of learning that emphasized the consequences of behavior. Skinner's notion of reinforcement is frequently applied in today's classrooms. Two types of *reinforcement* exist: *positive* and *negative.* **Positive reinforcement** increases the rate of response. An example of positive reinforcement would be giving a piece of candy to a student when he raises his hand as opposed to speaking out of turn. **Negative reinforcement** is a stimulus that, when removed, strengthens behavior. Seat belt buzzers are an example of negative reinforcement because you elicit a response to stop the negative reinforcement.

Two types of **reinforcers** are available for use. **Primary reinforcers**, like food or water, affect behavior without having to be learned. **Generalized reinforcers**, such as money, acquire their power because of their association with primary reinforcers.

Schedules of reinforcement are associated with the classroom because students need the proper reinforcement to continue certain positive behaviors. Two major categories, **interval** (time) and **ratio** (number of responses) exist. Each of these categories has two options, fixed or variable.

- *Fixed interval:* The time of reinforcement is preset
  Educational implication: As deadlines approach, student activity increases
- *Variable interval:* Time between reinforcement varies
  *Educational implication: S*teady activity results
- *Fixed ratio:* Reinforcement depends upon a definite number of responses
  Educational implication: After reinforcement, activity slows

- *Variable ratio:* The number of responses needed for reinforcement varies.

  Educational implication: This type of reinforcement shows the greatest activity.

Models of Classroom Management

It is estimated that up to fifty percent of all teachers will leave the field of education within seven years. This attrition rate is mostly due to poor methods of classroom management. Several methods exist to guide you in your quest for appropriate management techniques. These methods cover an array of models from highly directive behaviorist techniques to democratic and nondirective, facilitative procedures.

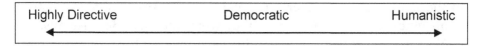

| Highly Directive | Democratic | Humanistic |

Figure 6.1 Models of Classroom Management

Highly directive models of classroom management.

Highly directive models occur when teachers direct students' behavior and control them with the use of external rewards and punishment. Instructional methods that accompany this model are lecturing, drill and practice, and questioning. Because few students are engaged at one time, this model has recently come under scrutiny.

Assertive discipline, an approach advocated by Lee Canter, is a behaviorist model of classroom management that maintains teachers have the right to establish rules, require student compliance, and expect parental and administrative support.

Behavior modification, a concept proposed by B. F. Skinner, is also highly directive. In this model, behavioral problems are defined and measured to determine what *antecedents* (triggers) or *consequences* (reinforcers) must be adjusted to successfully guide behavior. Punishment is an option in these models. Three types of acceptable punishments can be considered: private and consistently applied reprimands, time outs that remove the student from the reinforcing situation, and response cost,,,,,,,,,,, of which a token system is the most common.

Democratic models of classroom management.

Jacob Kounin's and Rudolf Dreikurs' theories of classroom management typify the *democratic model*. As its name implies, the democratic model allows students to participate in the management of the classroom.

Kounin maintained that teachers should prevent misbehavior rather than dealing with it once it occurs. His term, *with-it-ness*, applies to teachers who are consistently aware of what is occurring in the classroom. Students typically respect teachers who exemplify with-it-ness.

Kounin coined the term, the *ripple effect*. The ripple effect refers to the tendency for teacher reprimands or praises to spread to students other than those for which they were intended. Because misbehaviors are most likely to occur during transition times, Kounin encouraged teachers to maintain student focus by encouraging involvement. The greatest involvement occurs through the use of small group activities. During small group activities, teachers should make students accountable, have alerting cues and vary activities to prevent boredom.

Rudolf Dreikurs advocated *logical consequences* to misbehavior instead of punishment in his Democratic Model of classroom management. He believed that children make errors in their assumptions regarding what behaviors lead to desired goals. For example, often students who want attention get it by misbehaving. Teachers who give too much time and attention to misbehaviors are reinforcing the very behavior they want to diminish. For this reason, minor misconduct often ceases when teachers stop supporting the undesired behavior with attention. *Logical consequences* relate to the misconduct and seek to rectify the wrong. A policy requiring students to clean the room when they leave trash on the floor is an example of a logical consequence.

Harry Wong's democratic model advocates a businesslike approach. It is currently used in many induction programs. Learning students' names, explicitly teaching routines, and establishing a simple list of rules complete with consequences for violation and rewards for compliance, all combine to create an environment of security for students. According to Wong, both praise and criticism should be specific; teachers should praise students publicly, while criticism should be given privately.

Humanistic models of classroom management.

Humanistic models of classroom management are the most student-centered and the least directive in their approach. Carl Rogers advocated that students should have freedom to learn. According to Rogers, the goal for students is self-discipline, and teachers should be facilitators as opposed to directors. The instructional methods that accompany Roger's model are *inquiry learning*, *group projects*, and *self-assessment*. Students are viewed as important participants in the learning process. While Rogers did not advocate total permissiveness, he believed a list of rules would violate the autonomy of students. While the humanistic model communicates warmth and caring, it is not well suited for beginning teachers, as it lacks specific recommendations.

Current Trends in Classroom Management

Classroom management is a prerequisite to effective instruction. A well-designed environment with rules and routines facilitates the teaching and learning process. New teachers should initiate the process of managing their classroom by creating a mental checklist for the first day of a new school year. This will initially ensure that all aspects are addressed and that expectations are clearly communicated to students. Students who are aware of a teacher's expectations are less likely to make errors in judgment regarding acceptable behavior in that particular classroom. Current trends in classroom management consider the following classroom variables:

- Organizing the physical environment
- Creating classroom rules
- Consequences for misbehavior
- Rewards for rule compliance
- Creating classroom routines
- Transitions as routines
- Punishment

35

Organizing the physical environment.

What physical aspects of the classroom do you need to be aware of before the school year begins? Teachers must plan the classroom environment to facilitate learning. They need to anticipate the position of all classroom variables: people, desks, postings and materials.

Positioning people:

- All students should have a clear view of instructional information.
- The teacher should have a clear view of all the students. Research has suggested that teachers tend to pay attention to and dialogue with the first row across the classroom and the center aisle going back into the classroom, creating a T-pattern. To alleviate this trend and increase control, teachers should circulate around the classroom.

Desks and seating:

- Desks should initially be arranged facing the teacher so that he has the students' attention.
- Desk arrangement should facilitate activities after the first few days: a circle for group conversation or a group of four to five desks for small group work.
- Assign seating on the first day of school by displaying a graphic on an overhead projector, or in elementary school, place names on their desks. Seating assignments assist in learning students' names, taking roll and separating potential behavior problems.

Postings on walls:

- Post rules with consequences and rewards.
- Bulletin boards should be attractive and readied for student work or instructional aids to be displayed.
- Place daily assignments in a designated spot for students to see and anticipate.
- Record past assignments on a calendar for reference by students who were absent.
- Display an evacuation map for fires or other emergency procedures.

Materials:

- Materials such as pencil sharpeners, trash baskets, and books should be located where students can easily get to them without disturbing seated students.
- All materials that present a distraction should be located where students do not continually see them. For example, a science room that has animals should locate them in the back of the classroom.

Creating classroom rules.

Selected classroom rules should be in sync with existing school rules and the developmental stage of your students. Rules should be posted on the first day of school, and parents should be made aware of them through a mailing or a letter that is sent home with the students on the first day.

Students can be incorporated into the rule process by having them provide a rationale for the existence of the rule. While democratic models of classroom management might suggest children participate in the rule-making process, recent research indicates that teacher validity is enhanced when that teacher initially assumes the role of instructional leader determining the rules. Students may later share control after proving an appreciation of their responsibility to the group.

Rules should be presented in a positive manner and limited in number from three to five. Rewards for compliance and consequences for noncompliance to the rules should be posted. Consistency is key in implementation. If the teacher does not consistently follow the rules, why should students? Consistency in implementing the rules creates a secure environment for your students. Students can trust teachers who follow through on their word.

Consequences for misbehavior.

Stages of consequences for noncompliance to the rules should move from less to more severe. Consequences should start with a warning or cueing that the behavior is unacceptable. After an initial warning, a teacher might meet with the student to discuss the situation. As a third possible step, a telephone call home to the student's parent or guardian would be appropriate. In the event that the student fails to respond to these first techniques, developing a contract with the student might be necessary. Contracts should include the following items:

- The previous infraction
- The desired behavior
- Specific rewards for following the desired behavior
- Specific consequences for continued misbehavior
- The student's signature indicating an understanding of and compliance with the document

The student and teacher discuss the contents of the contract before the student signs it. A logical consequence to breaking the contract is administrative action. Even when an administrator becomes involved, teachers should be part of the process. Students perceive teachers who do not address their own students' discipline issues as incompetent.

Rewards for rule compliance.

Rewards for following the rules are initially important to motivate students but become less important as students realize the intrinsic satisfaction of a harmonious classroom. Ideally, the **Premack principle** can be applied. The Premack principle states that a preferred activity can be used as a positive reinforcer for a less frequent or less preferred activity. This means a teacher can use a reward that the student naturally engages in as a reinforcer: extra time on the playground, a few minutes at the end of class to socialize, or access to materials or activities that typically are not available.

Creating classroom routines.

It has been said that *the person with the best plan wins in a competition*. If a teacher does not have a plan for routines in the classroom, the students will develop their own methods. Discipline only becomes necessary when the routines of the classroom are not clearly stated and followed. The key to positive classroom management is to determine the necessary procedures and routines before the students arrive.

Once the school year begins, several days should be spent explaining the procedures and practicing the routines. Consider how you would have your students perform the following routines:

- Entering the room
- Exiting the room
- Asking questions
- Handing in school work
- Sharpening pencils
- Going to the restroom
- Responding to an emergency drill
- Forming cooperative learning groups

Transitions as routines.

Transition times occur when students move from one activity to another. Behavioral problems are most likely to occur during transition times. Routines must be established for transitions to increase instructional time and decrease possible behavior problems.

The beginning of the day in elementary school, or the start of a class in secondary school, must be managed. An activity that settles students and focuses their attention is advised: a discussion of the day's events with elementary students, or a problem on the board for secondary students.

Making students aware of the next assignment can lessen talking during transition times. By posting the days activities in a particular location within the classroom, you can accustom the students to looking for and following the schedule.

Punishment.

The need for punishment is currently viewed as a result of ineffective classroom management. Punishment, by definition, suppresses or weakens a behavior. While the elimination of a behavior may bring relief to a teacher, it tends to alienate the student from the teacher, undermining the learning process. Experts suggest that the following prevent punishment from being counterproductive to learning:

- Consequences for misbehavior must be established and shared with students at the beginning of the school year.

- Punishment should be applied consistently to similar misbehaviors.
- Punishment should be carried out privately so as not to provide a forum for attention or embarrass students.
- Positive alternative behaviors should be suggested.

When students are aware of consequences and they misbehave, they have chosen to experience the consequences. Although teachers are responsible for carrying out the penalty of misbehavior, students should be reminded that they made the decision to misbehave. Teachers act in a fair and equitable manner by following through with established consequences. Students can then trust that their classroom is an orderly and predictable environment. Three types of punishment are typically used in schools today:

- *Time out:* punishment that excludes students from activities and positive consequences
- *Response cost:* punishment that involves the loss of a positive reinforcer
- *Overcorrection:* the student receives consequences and also must display positive practice

CHAPTER 7

INSTRUCTIONAL DESIGN

What constitutes an effective lesson? Teaching strategies and instructional design are two elements that contribute to the success of lessons. When the message is clear, well organized, linked to past knowledge, and cognitively appropriate, learning will occur.

The goal of instruction is the acquisition of skills and knowledge by students. Increasingly, schools are also focusing on the ability to transfer those acquired skills and knowledge to life outside the school. *Transfer* occurs when students can successfully relate what they have learned in school to a new situation. Several factors impact the likelihood of transfer:

- Focusing on Standards and Objectives
- Utilizing All Levels of the Cognitive Taxonomy
- Implementing Various Methods of Instructional Delivery
- Creating Problem-Solving Opportunities

Focusing on Standards and Objectives

In most school districts, state or national standards drive the curriculum. Standards outline what students will be taught and what they should accomplish. Standards are organized into *scope* and *sequence*. Scope refers to the span of the curriculum, while sequence refers to the repetition and depth of content.

Instructional objectives are written by teachers to support standards. Instructional or learning objectives clearly state what the student is to accomplish. Objectives are written as part of the planning process so students know prior to the lesson what they are responsible for mastering. By using learning objectives, teachers can accurately assess student achievement.

Objectives assist in focusing you and your students on what they should be capable of performing at the end of instruction. Objectives can and should be modified to meet the needs of exceptional students and account for the cultural and experiential uniqueness of your own school's population. By connecting standards, learning objectives and assessment, you can achieve instructional alignment that maximizes effectiveness in teaching and learning.

Many teachers use four parts to write objectives, following an A, B, C, D format: the audience, the behavior expected of the student, the content in which learning occurs, and the degree of competency required:

- The *audience* is the student in a school setting. *The <u>student</u> will identify three characteristics of mammals with mastery.*
- The *behavior expected of the student* is always written in the form of a verb that indicates to the teacher that the student is capable of accomplishing the desired outcome. Examples of verbs that are observable are *define, describe, construct, classify, write, select, evaluate,* and *justify.* A teacher must be capable of observing or measuring the verbs that indicate the behavior expected of a student. *The student will <u>demonstrate</u> the use of a microscope by using slides with mastery.*
- The *content in which learning occurs* means the information with which students are working. *The student will define <u>the parts of speech in a story passage</u>.* The parts of speech in a story passage would be the content in which the student is working.
- The final element in an objective is the *degree of accuracy.* This simply means what level of competence a student is expected to display. *The student will list the vowels in the alphabet with <u>100% accuracy</u>.*

Standards and objectives comprise two components of a typical lesson plan. When you begin teaching, your school district will most likely provide a lesson plan format for you to follow. Most lesson plans contain the following:

- A listing of standards, objectives, materials, and necessary accommodations for diversity
- Methods for assessing prior knowledge, creating motivation, teaching the new skill or concept, practicing what was learned, and evaluating student learning

Utilizing All Levels of the Cognitive Taxonomy

Benjamin Bloom defined six levels of the cognitive domain that apply to what is traditionally thought of as *school learning.* **Bloom's Taxon-**

omy recognizes levels of understanding that proceed from lower-order thinking skills to higher-order thinking skills. This taxonomy is used to guide teachers as they assist students with initial understanding and eventually progress to higher-order thinking skills. The six levels of Bloom's cognitive taxonomy and their associated terms are:

- *Knowledge:* rote memorization of specifics
  Associated terms: select, define, reproduce, list
- *Comprehension:* explaining information in one's own words
  Associated terms: estimate, describe, classify, discuss
- *Application:* using information in an actual situation
  Associated terms: predict, solve, show, compute
- *Analysis:* examining the various parts of information
  Associated terms: infer, separate, point out, diagram
- *Synthesis:* constructing something unique by combining information
  Associated terms: adapt, rearrange, construct, devise
- *Evaluation:* appraising information or data
  Associated terms: judge, conclude, critique, defend

Knowledge and comprehension are considered as lower-order thinking skills, while application, analysis, synthesis, and evaluation are considered higher-order thinking skills. While students typically use the lower-order thinking skills when becoming familiar with new information, teachers should design lessons that require students to also utilize higher-order thinking skills. Both types of thinking skills should be incorporated when developing learning objectives.

Implementing Various Methods of Instructional Delivery

Instructional strategies can be divided into two major categories: *direct instruction,* a teacher-centered strategy, and *student-centered instruction,* which focuses on guiding students to construct their own understanding. Traditionally, models of teacher-centered instruction have prevailed in the classroom. However, current research indicates student-centered instruction that considers students' prior knowledge, learning styles, affective thoughts, and social or cultural environment maximizes effectiveness. You should familiarize yourself with these common delivery methods:

- Direct instruction
- Student-centered instruction

Direct instruction.

Direct instruction is a teacher-centered approach that focuses on learning objectives, incorporating well-defined content with teacher-guided instruction. Many scholastic concepts are initially introduced with this method. The major models of direct instruction all share four essential steps:

- An introduction and review of prior experience or knowledge to focus attention and motivate students
- A presentation of information that might include examples, modeling, and an assessment of comprehension
- Guided practice with supervision and scaffolding (support for gaps in understanding) provided by the teacher or other students
- Independent practice to review and increase competence

Direct instruction has both its critics and its advocates. Critics argue that direct instruction focuses on Bloom's lower-level thinking skills and fails to maintain the complexity of an authentic environment by fragmenting content. Advocates of this teacher-centered approach suggest it is one of the most effective methods for initially exposing students to concepts or instructing students with cognitive or academic difficulties.

Student-centered instruction.

Student-centered approaches to instruction have gained popularity with the rise of *constructivism.* Constructivism is a theory of how individuals gain knowledge. Simply stated, this view maintains that students construct their knowledge from their experiences through interaction with the environment. Students must then actually have experiences to construct knowledge as opposed to merely listening to lectures.

Student-centered instruction requires teachers to provide learning situations and environments that guide students to develop authentic and transferable understanding. Students can then actively participate in the process of knowledge construction. Goals and objectives continue to drive instruction in this model.

The ability to implement student-centered instruction hinges on maintaining an orderly environment where students are aware of the teacher's expectations and the goals of instruction. Five major types of student-centered instruction exist:

- Discovery learning
- Inquiry method
- Cooperative learning
- Individualized instruction
- Technology

Discovery learning, associated with Jerome Bruner, occurs when a teacher organizes the class so students can learn by becoming actively involved. At the preschool level, students may experience *unguided discovery* when little or no direction is provided. In the elementary and secondary school, teachers should initiate *guided discovery*: direction is given by providing a provoking question or scenario to encourage students to explore for answers and explanations.

Inquiry learning is associated with John Dewey. In this model, students formulate a hypothesis, collect data, draw conclusions, and reflect and evaluate. Often associated with science, the inquiry model allows students to gain knowledge of content and process it simultaneously.

Cooperative learning occurs when students work in small mixed-ability groups that encourage total participation. This model assists students in developing a sense of interdependence, encourages relationships, and facilitates the development of communication, leadership, and conflict management. The success of cooperative learning depends upon how well teachers communicate their expectations, organize student routines, and monitor the process. The following guidelines are offered for successful cooperative learning experiences:

- Groups should be of mixed ability.
- Placement in groups is determined by the students' capacity to work together.

- Common goals should be established with clear guidelines on outcomes and behavior provided.
- Individual tasks are delegated to encourage group interdependence.
- The length of time should be predetermined.
- Final assessment must encompasses both the performance of the individual and the group.

Cooperative learning has many advantages. Academically, this model benefits students by providing peer scaffolding, increased opportunities for involvement, and an enhanced ability to problem solve by exposing students to the perspectives of others. Socially, cooperative learning promotes the acceptance of gender, ethnic, and academic diversity.

Individualized instruction is designed to meet the specific needs of a particular student. This type of variation on typical instruction may modify time, activities, or materials. This method is often employed with students who have special needs or those who are gifted.

Technology is the latest addition to the student-centered repertoire of instructional techniques. Videotapes, computers, calculators, and the Internet provide many opportunities for students to practice skills, research or explore topics, and interact with peers. However visually engaging and critically important for participation in today's society, the application of technology to instruction does not guarantee improved learning. Teachers must establish and clearly communicate the goals of learning when utilizing technology in the classroom.

Creating problem-solving opportunities.

When students construct concepts and apply them to problematic situations, they are said to be *problem solving*. Teachers who design problem-solving situations that resemble the world outside the classroom increase the likelihood of students transferring their ability to other problem-solving situations. The two general categories of problem-solving situations are **well-defined** (or well-structured) and **ill-defined** (or ill-structured).

Well-defined problems:

- Goals are clear.
- All information is present
- There is one path to a solution

Ill-defined problems:

- Goals may be unclear.
- Relevant information may be missing.
- Several solutions might exist.

Providing opportunities for students to engage in ill-defined problem-solving situations is better for transfer because most problems outside of the school environment are ill defined.

Two general approaches to solving problems are **algorithms** and **heuristics**. Algorithms use a step-by-step approach, much like directions for assembling a product. A heuristic approach is a general strategy that may or may not yield a definite solution. One heuristic model is the **DUPE method**. In this scenario students proceed through the following steps:

- Define the problem.
- Understand the various facets of the problem.
- Plan for a solution.
- Evaluate the outcome.

CHAPTER 8

MOTIVATION

How will you motivate students to learn? Motivation is a force that stimulates, maintains, and directs an individual's behavior toward a goal. Motivation is correlated with achievement; motivated students persist, take risks, and cause fewer discipline problems. A comprehensive review of motivation in preparation for the *Principles of Learning and Teaching* exam explores the following subjects:

- Extrinsic and Intrinsic Motivation
- Maslow's Hierarchy of Needs
- Attribution Theory
- Learning Goals Versus Performance Goals
- Modeling

Extrinsic and Intrinsic Motivation

The two general categories of motivation are *extrinsic* and *intrinsic motivation*. Extrinsic motivation, as the name implies, is a student's response to external stimuli. Intrinsic motivation occurs when a student engages in an activity for its own sake.

Extrinsic motivation.

Extrinsic motivation frequently takes the form of reinforcement. In the behaviorist model, the teacher employs rewards to increase a certain behavior. A wide variety of extrinsic rewards exist: teacher praise, consumable items, grades, or using reinforcement that students would select naturally, such as extra recess or social time (*Premack principle*).

While initially useful to motivate an unmotivated student or group of students, extrinsic reinforcement has received criticism. Research indicates that the goal-driven behavior created by external reinforcement decreases the interest in the task itself by creating a focus on the reward. However, extrinsic reinforcement can be legitimately employed in the following scenarios:

- To engage students in an activity or task of low interest
- To provide feedback for increasing competence

- To give students social support and acceptance

Once students experience success in a task or activity, the goal for a teacher is to decrease extrinsic reinforcers and refocus students on the intrinsic satisfaction of a job well done.

Intrinsic motivation.

Intrinsic motivation typically occurs during activities that are characterized as affective, challenging, personally selected, or highly novel. When students feel internally rewarded through the activities themselves, they are said to be experiencing intrinsic motivation. Ideally, teachers should create learning situations that evoke intrinsic reinforcement.

Maslow's Hierarchy of Needs

Motivation to learn can be affected by events or situations beyond the classroom. While you cannot be held accountable for controlling all aspects of your students' lives, you need to be aware of the relationship between needs and motivation. Abraham Maslow's Hierarchy of Needs examines the relationship between motivation and learning.

Maslow's Hierarchy of Needs reminds teachers that personal needs must be met before students can concentrate on intellectual pursuits. The pyramid contains seven steps grouped into *deficiency needs* and *growth needs*. Deficiencies must be met before an individual can concentrate on growth needs. There are four deficiency steps in the pyramid beginning with the most basic of needs and progressing to those needs less vital:

- *Physiological needs:* food, shelter and water
- *Safety needs:* freedom from physical or emotional harm
- *Belonging needs:* love and acceptance from peers and family
- *Self-esteem needs:* recognition and approval from those considered important to an individual

According to Maslow, these needs must be met before one can proceed unhindered to the growth needs. The growth needs consist of:

- Intellectual achievement
- Aesthetic appreciation
- Self-actualization

In the self-actualized state, individuals are capable of great insight, creativity and acceptance.

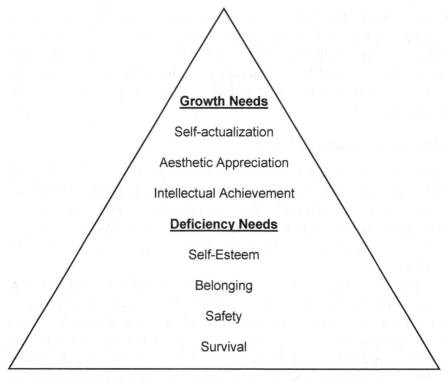

Figure 8.1 Maslow's Hierarchy of Needs

Solutions to deficiency needs.

Schools have developed programs and relationships to cope with the deficiency needs of survival and safety:

- Free or reduced-cost meal programs for low-income students
- Collaborative relationships with social service agencies, that increase the well being of students at the institutional level
- Sponsored school programs to assist and provide guidance for students facing personal challenges such as bullying

Within the classroom, teachers can provide for the deficits in belonging and self-esteem by creating an atmosphere of interrelatedness and carefully selecting learning activities:

- Be available for students and empathize with their concerns.
- Create learning activities that build relationships among students.
- Select developmentally appropriate assignments in which students can experience success.

Once students experience the delight of success, they are often motivated to take on additional academic challenges and risks. By addressing deficit needs of students, schools and teachers free students to engage in intellectual pursuits.

Attribution Theory

Attribution theory is an effort to account for why students are either successful or unsuccessful in the classroom. Students can either attribute their success or lack of it to themselves or to causes external to them. When students believe their success or failure lies within their control, they are said to have an internal locus of control. They believe that with the necessary instruction and the right amount of effort, they can experience success. Individuals with an internal locus of control exhibit the following characteristics:

- Take responsibility for their outcomes
- Experience pride for their successes
- Exhibit autonomy in their endeavors
- Tend to attribute failure to a lack of effort

When faced with failure, students with an internal locus of control increase their efforts and ultimately achieve success. Motivation, in this case, spurs the student to achieve what is possible.

Unlike the student who has an internal locus of control, other students believe that external events determine their success in the classroom. These students are said to have an *external locus of control*. Teachers can identify students with an external locus of control by observing how they credit or blame their performance.

If a student uses the following excuses, chances are they have an external locus of control:

- Luck
- Lack of innate ability
- An external uncontrollable cause

In this scenario, because students cannot take personal credit for academic events, motivation is decreased and effort is perceived as unrelated to success. Many students who exhibit learned helplessness, the sentiment that no amount of effort can lead to achievement, have an external locus of control. At-risk students frequently have a history of attributing their lack of academic success to factors outside their control, thus resulting in a lack of motivation and persistence.

To combat the cycle created by learned helplessness and an external locus of control, research indicates that teachers should train students to realize the connection between effort and learning. Teachers need to design challenging activities and ensure that students have the necessary tools for success. Once students experience a positive outcome and can attribute it to their own effort, motivation for future endeavors is increased.

As success continues, students can develop a sense of *self-efficacy*, a belief that they are capable or competent to perform certain tasks or activities. Self-efficacy is influenced by successful past performance.

Learning Goals Versus Performance Goals

Motivation for students to stretch and learn new skills is frequently influenced by how they perceive their present competence in that arena. For example, students who lack physical coordination are often not motivated to engage in physical education activities due to what they view as poor past performances.

- *Performance goals:* a student's desire to look good or avoid looking inept to others
- *Learning goals:* a student's desire to master additional skills or attain new information

Teachers should assist students in setting learning goals. Students who establish learning goals for themselves, or are encouraged by their teachers to do so, view the learning process as a personal endeavor. Students who have learning goals exhibit the following qualities:

- Tend to persevere because they realize accomplishments come with effort
- Exhibit self-regulatory behavior
- Use their teachers as resources

Conversely, students who have performance goals look outward for validation of their competence. These students are likely to cheat, compare their performance with others, seek attention for their performance, and focus on grades instead of the acquisition of knowledge.

Teachers can encourage the pursuit of learning goals that favorably influence the motivation to learn. Initially, students should be encouraged to set specific, moderately challenging, realistic learning goals. Teacher feedback can then provide students with their present level of competence and guidance on how to attain the desired level of competence. The focus must be on improvement as opposed to final performance.

Modeling

Modeling occurs when individuals change as a result of observing another's actions. Modeling can be an effective method of motivation. Teachers influence this type of motivation by showcasing successful models and exhibiting positive attitudes.

Teachers can encourage students to have pride in their cultural background, exceptionalities, or gender by using models. Peer modeling is another useful tool for teachers. In the classroom, students witnessing a similar other successfully performing a task often feel that they too are capable of performing that task.

Teachers have the potential to be positive models for their students. Their beliefs and attitudes are communicated to students through modeling. Teachers who are enthusiastic, with a desire to learn, inspire their students to exhibit those same qualities. Research indicates that student performance improves when teachers have positive expectations.

CHAPTER 9

SPECIAL EDUCATION

As a regular classroom teacher you will likely have *inclusion* students. These students with special needs have the protection of federal legislation and unique educational requirements.

Questions on the *Principles of Learning and Teaching* exam reflect this increased focus on creating an instructional environment that provides positive experiences for all students. There are several issues with which you must familiarize yourself:

- Legal Aspects of Special Education
- Legal Implications for General Education Teachers
- General Classifications of Students with Special Needs

Legal Aspects of Special Education

Public Law 94-142, passed in 1975, required states to provide a free and appropriate public education for every child between the ages of three and twenty-one—if free public education is provided by the state to children of those ages—regardless of handicap or severity of handicap. Today the law has been extended to provide services for all children with disabilities from birth to twenty-one years of age and requires an *individualized education program (IEP)* for students age three to twenty-one with disabilities.

In 1997, the Individuals with Disabilities Education Act (IDEA) stated that educational rights are to be granted to all people from birth to age twenty-one who have cognitive, emotional, or physical disabilities. This law also guarantees the following five rights for students with disabilities:

- A free and appropriate public education (FAPE)
- Fair and nondiscriminatory evaluation
- An individualized education program (IEP)
- An education in the least restrictive environment (LRE)
- Due process

Identification and evaluation.

Presently, the IDEA advocates a step-by-step process to ensure that needs of students with exceptionalities are met. Referral to special education programs can come from parents, teachers, or physicians. The school and the parents must agree to testing. This initial referral determines whether the student is eligible for special education services.

Evaluation of the student must be nondiscriminatory, multidisciplinary, and comprehensive. All areas that can possibly impact the educational setting are tested. If testing determines that the student qualifies for special education services, an IEP is developed. Identification and labeling of students with special needs is important:

- Teachers can make generalizations regarding choices involving social and academic development.
- Social and political interest groups can promote and support the special interests of students receiving special education services.
- Federal funds are only provided when students have been identified as having special needs.

Individualized education programs.

An IEP exists as a guide for educational achievement and includes the following:

- Present level of performance
- Strengths and needs
- Annual goals and short-term objectives
- Instructional strategies
- Support services
- Evaluating criteria

There are several participants in the IEP process: the student's parents, a general education teacher, a school administrator, a special education teacher, and an IEP specialist, who can also be one of the previously mentioned members of the team. When appropriate, students who are fourteen or older should also be encouraged to take part in their IEP meetings. The IEP provides the student's teachers with the student's present level, unique needs, necessary modifications or related services, goals and objectives, and transition planning.

Placement.

A continuum of placement possibilities exists for special education students. The least restrictive environment (LRE) mandated by the IDEA advocates that students should be placed in the general classroom setting if their academic, physical and social needs can be satisfied there. This type of placement is referred to as *inclusion.*

In the inclusive setting, special education students are placed in the regular classroom and are provided with the necessary support services to ensure success. The current definition of inclusion requires individualization for all students and involves cooperating teachers in which two teachers, regular education and special education, teach all students.

Research has shown that many special education students achieve at a higher rate when placed in settings with nondisabled classmates. Additional benefits that have also been cited include: improved classroom behavior, opportunities to interact with nondisabled peers, enhanced self-image, and improved attitude toward school.

Modifications.

Teachers in the inclusive setting must implement the student's IEP, making modifications to ensure success when indicated or necessary. A variety of modification possibilities for assignments and testing exist:

- Adjust the size of assignments
- Vary the time allowed
- Increase the amount of support provided
- Decrease the level of difficulty
- Alter the extent of participation
- Provide an alternative assignment that capitalizes on a student's strengths

Special education services are also provided for gifted students. Although the federal government does not mandate such services, many states do require gifted education be provided. Gifted students' assignments should also be modified to provide them with stimulating challenges that may involve acceleration.

Currently, the largest groups of students receiving special education services are those with learning disabilities, followed by those with communication disorders, mental retardation, and behavior disorders.

Legal Implications for General Education Teachers

As the number of students with IEPs increases, so do the legal implications for teachers and school districts. The law mandates specific provisions for students and the parents of students in special education. *Due process* serves as a safeguard. It guarantees the involvement of parents in the placement of their child. Due process also specifies parents have access to their child's school records, an opportunity for independent evaluation, the right to an interpreter if needed, and reimbursement for legal fees if a parent prevails in a lawsuit against a school or district.

What does this mean for you as a general education teacher with inclusion students in your classroom? Teachers are responsible for following through with IEPs. By implementing IEPs, general education teachers draw upon the strengths and adequately compensate for weaknesses of students with exceptionalities thereby increasing success. By making learning a positive and rewarding experience, you encourage future learning. This positive cycle is important for all students and is especially vital for those students who have obstacles, to overcome.

In addition to your academic responsibilities, students receiving special education services may need additional assistance in the social realm. By clearly defining behavioral expectations, you ensure success for students with special needs. The classroom should be predictable and orderly. Consequences and rewards must be consistently applied. To encourage positive social interaction between students with special needs and those in general education, teachers may employ peer tutoring and cooperative learning groups.

General Classifications of Students with Special Needs

The *Principles of Learning and Teaching* exam requires you to be familiar with several areas of exceptionalities. Listed below are the five major areas of exceptionalities, their defining characteristics, their most commonly occurring manifestations, and suggested classroom strategies.

Cognitive or academic challenges:

- *Characteristics:* Challenges in specific cognitive processes such as memory, language, or perception
- *Manifestations:* Learning disabilities, speech and communication disorders, attention deficit hyperactivity disorder
- *Strategies:* Implement the IEP, create routines, limit distractions, analyze students' work to identify and assist with specific challenges

Social or behavioral challenges:

- *Characteristics:* Exhibit behaviors that are disruptive and/or notably disrupt academic performance
- *Manifestations:* Autism and behavioral disorders
- *Strategies:* Implement the IEP, create routines, limit distractions, establish clear guidelines for interaction, employ cooperative learning and peer tutoring, limit unsupervised activities

Delays in cognitive and social performance:

- *Characteristics:* Considerably below average intelligence and insufficient adaptive behavior
- *Manifestations:* Mental retardation
- *Strategies:* Implement the IEP, create routines, establish reasonable goals, use direct instruction and peer tutoring

Physical or sensory difficulties:

- *Characteristics:* Medical or physical conditions of the body or senses
- *Manifestations:* Hearing or visual impairments or loss, and health or physical difficulties

- *Strategies:* Implement the IEP, provide a means for participation, and utilize technology to assist with instructional goals

Advanced cognitive development:

- *Characteristics:* Advanced intellectual ability or talents
- *Manifestations:* Giftedness
- *Strategies:* Implement the IEP, encourage autonomy by teaching research strategies, and promote the use of higher-order thinking skills

CHAPTER 10

STUDENT ASSESSMENT

Two sections of the *Principles of Learning and Teaching* exam require that, as a future teacher, you understand many facets of student assessment. Assessment guides educators in decisions regarding future instruction; at the state and national levels, assessment takes the form of standardized tests to compare populations of students at different schools. Just as making students aware of objectives before a lesson increases the likelihood of successfully obtaining those objectives, the more familiar you are with the various forms of assessment, the more useful they will be to you.

Three types of assessment exist: *diagnostic, formative* and *summative*. Diagnostic assessment provides information needed to make decisions regarding alternative methods or procedures. Diagnosis means determining the content or type of instruction needed for a student or students. Formative evaluation determines what students know and can do prior to, or during, instruction. Summative testing assesses students' achievement upon the completion of a lesson or unit of work.

High stakes exist in testing. High performing school districts receive positive press, while those that perform poorly are threatened by the state with losing their autonomy. This review of assessment will begin with what you can do as a classroom teacher and extend to standardized testing performed nationally:

- Testing Terminology
- Types of Assessment
- Norm-Referenced and Criterion-Referenced Scoring
- Communicating with Students

Testing Terminology

Quality testing shares four characteristics. Reliability, standardization, validity, and practicality are all necessary components for high quality testing instruments.

Reliability alludes to the consistency of test scores. If the scores from a test are highly consistent, teachers have a valid basis for using the scores to determine students' general understanding of the concepts taught. When scores fluctuate wildly, the degree of reliability is said to diminish.

Standardization may improve the objectivity of tests. It refers to the degree to which testing procedures are kept uniform. When administrative tasks, equipment, materials, observation, and scoring rules are consistent, testing is then referred to as standardized.

Validity refers to the extent that the test measures what it claims to measure. The validity of assessment depends on the purpose and context of its intended use. An assessment instrument may be valid for some purposes and less valid for others.

Practicality, as the name implies, alludes to the ease of implementation and the investment or cost of the assessment. Of the four terms associated with assessment, practicality rates as the newest consideration.

Types of Assessment

You will assess students in your classroom for many reasons. Tests assist teachers in decision making and serve as a means of improving instruction. Objective, content-based tests and essays have traditionally been used in the classroom. Performance based assessment methods have recently gained favor. In the following sections the defining features and the advantages and disadvantages of all three types of classroom assessment are explained:

- Objective Assessment
- Essays
- Performance-based Assessment

Objective assessment.

Objective assessment determines the core knowledge students have of a subject. *Declarative knowledge*, or knowledge of how things are, such as vocabulary, fundamental concepts, and basic procedural means, can be assessed through objective tests. These tests require students to answer questions, problem solve, or provide responses on paper. Ideally, these types of tests should represent course objectives.

Teacher-designed objective tests have a variety of uses. Summative (accumulative) judgments and formative evaluations can result.

When they are used to assign grades, objective tests assume the role of summative evaluation. Objective tests can also be used as a means of formative assessment to improve learning and teaching, and can determine the following:

- Establish student readiness
- Judge the effectiveness of instruction
- Identify learning difficulties
- Determine prior knowledge
- Provide motivation for students to learn

Objective tests have remained popular for several reasons:

- Reliability is high
- Objectivity is high
- Scoring can be performed electronically
- Large numbers of students can be assessed easily

There are many drawbacks to objective tests. The incidence of transfer of knowledge decreases when the environment of assessment is unlike the real world. Objective tests lack the complexity associated with actual performance. The best use of objective tests is in the beginning of instruction to establish a base of core knowledge that is highly structured, skill based, or literal.

Essay tests.

Essay tests require students to provide explanations. Students must organize their responses, but they experience greater freedom with regard to their responses than in objective tests. While essay tests take less time to construct, they require an investment of time to grade. Scoring can be highly subjective.

For transfer purposes, essay tests receive higher marks than their objective counterparts. Essay tests that require students to use higher-order thinking skills, such as analysis, synthesis, evaluation, or justification, increase the likelihood of transfer. Students in this scenario must interact with the information by interpreting or elaborating. Through interaction, knowledge connections stored in long-term memory increase and are available in the future for transfer to similar or generalized situations.

Performance-based assessment.

Performance-based assessment is used to determine if students can perform an activity or action as an indicator of academic competence. *Procedural knowledge*, or how to do things, is best evaluated by *performance-based assessment*. Frequently referred to as *authentic assessment* when used in a real world context, performance assessment emphasizes students' active responses that result in a product or event. The term *authenticity* gained favor with the increased focus on transfer. The more the activity resembles the real world, the more likely the information learned in the school setting will transfer to the environment beyond the classroom.

Ideally, a performance-based assessment activity should reflect what those in the field of study do. Whether building an engine in auto mechanics, participating in an archeological dig in history, or driving a car in drivers' education, performance assessment has proven to be highly motivating in schools that use it.

Portfolio assessment is related to performance assessment. As an assembled collection of work, a portfolio chronicles a student's abilities. Teachers encourage students to reflect on their performance and improve works that are of particular interest to them. Much like the world of work, students take an active role in assessing their performance and adjusting products. Process takes precedent in this type of performance assessment.

Performance assessment and portfolios can obtain a high degree of objectivity if a predetermined scoring *rubric* or criterion is established. Just as objectives focus students in lessons, establishing a rubric that informs students how various performances equate to grades will guide students to desired outcomes.

Norm-referenced and Criterion-referenced Scoring

Experts in test construction develop standardized tests. Most frequently found in the form of achievement tests, they generally assess the academic progress of students. Standardized testing has come under scrutiny recently because of the scoring, specifically, as well as the equity and utility of the scoring.

Norm-referenced scores are accomplished by comparing the performance of students. These types of scores do not tell teachers what has or has not been learned, but they do compare populations. When scores are norm-referenced, the scores are spread out so that even if all the students in the class received high grades, the lower of the high grades would appear in the lower quartile. If improperly explained to parents (making them think it reflects their child's grade), norm-referenced test scores can be alarming. As schools move toward community oriented models, norm-referenced testing is viewed as less favorable than criterion-referenced testing because it encourages competition rather than cooperation among students.

Most states have adopted tests that utilize *criterion-referenced* scoring. Student evaluation is based on a set criterion in this type of test, not on the performance of others. Sometimes referred to as *mastery tests*, criterion-referenced scores can be used by teachers to determine whether students have attained predetermined knowledge and skills. In an environment where state standards drive district curriculum, this type of scoring makes sense.

Standards give rise to specific objectives and these objectives in turn are easily assessed by criterion-referenced tests. The focus in this environment is success for all, not comparisons.

Communicating with Students

In the past your teachers probably kept test items secret. We now have a better understanding of learning and retention. By sharing objectives and assessment methods with students, learning and retention improve and anxiety decreases. Students become partners in this modern paradigm of instruction. Plan to use the four following suggestions when incorporating students into the assessment process:

- Show students that learning objectives and assessment directly relate
- Supply students with models of work and rubrics
- Encourage students to monitor their progress
- Allow students to revise or retake assessments

Assessment ideally measures students' future ability. By including students in this process, you encourage an internal locus of control. Students then realize the connection between their choices and their future.

CHAPTER 11

TEACHER PROFESSIONALISM

As the bar is raised for teacher candidates, so is the level of esteem associated with those in the field. With the increased focus on teaching as a profession, society has expectations concerning the amount of expertise professional teachers demonstrate. Today's professional teachers must familiarize themselves with four major areas:

- Current Trends
- Responsibility in Education
- Teacher Accountability
- Effective Communication

Current Trends

Increasingly the educational community is coming to terms with the notion that the student must be at the center of learning. The focus is on creating environments and personalizing instruction to facilitate learning and ensure student success.

Creating special environments.

Schools are expanding to provide authentic learning environments for their students. Apprenticeships are opportunities for students to plan and problem solve with an expert in a particular field. Mentor programs pair students with successful individuals who can teach those qualities to the student. Increasingly, traditional schools are placing students in settings that either simulate or are the actual environment where skills learned are practiced. For example, students might test water resources in the community for the level of purity or contamination. These attempts at authenticity increase the likelihood of transfer.

Magnet schools, charter schools, and cyber schools also give students an alternative to a typical public school environment. Magnet schools, or centers, provide a special curriculum designed to attract students of various racial backgrounds. Designed to remedy segregation, magnet schools are capable of reassigning students and faculty to prevent minority group isolation in school districts. They are typified by a specialty curriculum, such as science, foreign language, or the performing arts, which is not offered in depth in the same district. Research indicates that magnet schools actually do little to increase integration.

Charter schools developed as an attempt by teachers, parents, and community members to provide a stimulating and effective learning environment for students. These schools are autonomous and independent of the regulations and rules that govern the traditional public school system. The success of the charter school movement is largely due to community support, involving parents, community groups, universities, and business. Charter schools must demonstrate their effectiveness or their charters are revoked. Research has shown that these schools have somewhat homogenous populations and lack consistent systems devised for accountability.

Cyber schools are the latest addition to alternative instructional environments. These Internet-based schools lend themselves to secondary curriculums with students who have already acquired fundamental academic skills. Cyber schools are particularly suitable for students who cannot function in the traditional environment due to health or behavioral problems.

Personalizing instruction.

Instructional strategies have also expanded to accommodate the individual student, capitalizing on learning styles and talents. One strategy, *differentiated instruction,* considers the unique abilities of each student. In this model, you as a teacher recognize student differences and plan instruction accordingly. Differentiated instruction requires educators to attain a large repertoire of instructional methods and also have a complete understanding of content knowledge. The rationale for this current trend lies in the belief that the more successful and fulfilling learning experiences are for students, the more motivated they will be to learn. An additional way to adapt instruction and facilitate learning is to accommodate students' learning styles. Traditionally, three methods of delivery have been encouraged: *visual, auditory,* and *kinesthetic.* Because students have various preferences for receiving information, a combination approach using all three types of stimulation is recommended.

The notion of using learning styles and preferences to increase motivation has broadened to encompass students' talents. Howard Gardner developed a theory of *multiple intelligences.* Although school learning typically draws upon only two types of intelligences, linguistic and logical-mathematical, Gardner proposed that other facets of intelligence exist and teachers should draw on these to support and celebrate diversity. The theory of multiple intelligences encourages teachers to discover these talents in their students and capitalize on these strengths. This shift away from a *deficit model*—focusing on students' shortcomings—to a model that capitalizes on students' abilities is yet another attempt by schools to create environments for students that lead to positive experiences and feelings. Nine of the multiple intelligences are listed here:

- *Linguistic intelligence:* the capacity to use language effectively
- *Logical-mathematical intelligence:* the ability to think logically, especially in science and math
- *Spatial intelligence:* accurately perceiving visual images and imagined representations
- *Musical intelligence:* sensitivity to the creation and appreciation of music
- *Bodily-kinesthetic intelligence:* reveals itself in physical ability
- *Interpersonal intelligence:* the ability to understand the behaviors of others
- *Intrapersonal intelligence:* an understanding of your own feelings and beliefs
- *Naturalist intelligence:* an awareness of the similarities and differences found in the natural world
- *Existential intelligence:* the inclination to reflect upon the qualities that make humans unique

Responsibility in Education

The public school system in America is controlled by individual states. Typically, a state department of education selects and monitors state standards and assessment. Locally, district school boards work with superintendents and administrators to establish and implement the policies that drive the daily operations of schools. At a building level, principals operate their buildings, and teachers implement the policies determined by the state and district by instructing students. As a teacher, you can now participate in the decision making process in three important ways:

- School Based Management
- Legal Liability
- No Child Left Behind

School-based management.

In recent years, a movement has developed that is referred to as *site-based management* or *school-based management*. In this model, it is assumed that those at the building level have a certain amount of expertise concerning the needs and culture of their community and thus should have significant input on the policies that guide their school. In this decentralized model, teachers experience a high level of involvement, are given decision-making authority, and are accountable for outcomes. The goals of site-based management are improved student performance, heightened satisfaction of school level administration and teachers, and increased community involvement.

Legal liability.

Because teachers enjoy a high amount of autonomy in their classroom, it is paramount that they understand the laws that govern the participants in school systems. Just as American culture is characterized by change, so is the culture of the American school system. Research states that on any given day, 135,000 students bring guns to school. In special education, the number of students benefiting from programs grows every year and represents more than eleven percent of the entire school-age population. Legislation is addressed daily in an attempt to deal with these changes and to balance the rights of all participants in the school community:

- All states have laws mandating that teachers or administrators report cases of suspected child abuse.
- The Individuals with Disabilities Education Act (IDEA) states that educational rights are to be granted to all people from

birth to age twenty-one who have cognitive, emotional or physical disabilities.

- The IDEA also guarantees the following five rights for students with disabilities: a free and appropriate education (FAPE), fair and nondiscriminatory evaluation, an individualized education program (IEP), an education in the least restrictive environment (LRE) and due process.
- When interviewing for a position, teachers, administrators and other school staff are not required to give information unrelated to that position. This includes such aspects as age, marital status or religious affiliation.
- Freedom from discriminatory action applies to teachers and students; however, reverse discrimination is allowed in hiring faculty for the purpose of providing role models for culturally diverse populations.
- Freedom of speech applies to teachers and students unless the exercise of this constitutional right disrupts the learning process.
- Teachers are free to pursue their interests and affiliations outside of the institution regardless of the sentiments of their superiors, providing they act within the confines of the law and their activities do not negatively impact instructional performance.
- Teachers are responsible for the safety of students in their classroom and can be held accountable for negligent behavior.
- Most school districts have zero tolerance policies against the possession of illegal drugs or weapons on school grounds.
- Since states govern the laws regarding corporal punishment in public schools, teachers should familiarize themselves with the specific policies.

No Child Left Behind.

The *No Child Left Behind* (NCLB) Act, passed in 2001, requires that "all children have a fair, equal and significant opportunity to obtain a high quality education and reach, at a minimum, proficiency on challenging state academic achievement standards and state academic assessments" (No Child Left Behind Act, 2002). The six provisions of NCLB follow:

- Requiring accountability for results through state assessments
- Reducing federal, state, and local red tape to allow flexibility in spending federal funds
- Providing options for parents whose children are located in failing schools
- Ensuring that every child can read through increased federal funding for reading instruction
- Requiring a highly qualified teacher in every public school by 2005
- Promoting English proficiency by consolidating federal agencies which assist limited English proficient students

Teacher Accountability

The habits and talents you develop over the years contribute to accountability. School districts assist their teaching staff in their pursuit of increased competency and professionalism. This section contains current practices that will increase your competence and relay to others that you believe in accountability:

- Induction programs
- Self-reflection and evaluation

Induction programs.

Induction programs rose out of the need to address new teacher isolation. Induction programs help teachers successfully adjust to their new career in education. They furnish information regarding district resources, review effective pedagogical practices and reduce attrition rates. Typically, induction programs begin before the school year starts and can continue for as long as two years.

Self-reflection and evaluation.

An essential element of improvement is self-evaluation or reflection. Self-evaluation consists of a teacher evaluating their three main responsibilities: knowledge of subject matter, knowledge of curriculum (selected parts of the subject matter that is taught to students) and pedagogy (instructional strategies). Reflection implies that teachers review past situations, examine their choices, and assess how they might improve instruction for their students.

Once you enter the world of education, the opportunities for improved performance continue. The Praxis III consists of classroom performance assessments for practicing teachers. It exists as a guide for teachers, providing structure for improvements. Teacher evaluations for the Praxis III can take many forms, including observations, portfolios, videotape, and copies of student assignments or samples of a teacher's work.

The National Board for Professional Teaching Standards is another evaluative tool for experienced teachers. It provides teachers with an opportunity to receive advanced certification. Five areas are evaluated in this national assessment: commitment to students, knowledge of subject matter and pedagogy, classroom management, reflective thinking, and collaborative awareness.

Effective Communication

Positive communication habits are essential for successful teaching. Whether interacting with others in the field or with parents, the ability to create collaborative environments facilitates the teaching and learning process. When you begin your career, three major areas necessitate effective communication:

- Inclusion Students
- Parent Contact
- Conferencing

Inclusion students.

Inclusive classrooms necessitate communication. In addition to considering the typical needs of learning and participation, regular classroom teachers should incorporate individuals specifically trained in special education when planning for instruction. In inclusive settings, several opportunities for collaboration exist:

- Understanding a student's IEP
- Consulting and planning
- Coordinating assignments with resource room teachers

- Establishing a rapport and system for team teaching scenarios

Parent contact.

Communicating successfully with parents has many benefits. Attendance increases, students tend to exhibit positive attitudes, and academic achievement improves when parents are encouraged to participate in the education process.

Guidelines exist that increase the likelihood of positive interaction with parents and guardians. You should introduce yourself to parents with a telephone call or letter before the beginning of school. This initial positive contact paves the way for a continuing relationship. Once the school year begins, you should send a letter home describing classroom expectations and rules to parents. Learning communities in which all parties are well informed experience greater success. An additional note or letter home, updating parents on classroom events and projects, conveys to parents that their child's classroom is a productive learning environment.

Conferencing

Conferences are an excellent way to facilitate cooperation from parents. Whether the meeting is a scheduled conference time by the school or a negative situation exists, teachers must be well prepared. Teachers should arrive with grades, samples of work, and paper to take notes. When parents arrive for a conference, certain strategies help make parents feel positive and cooperative:

- Stand when parents arrive as a sign of recognition and respect.
- Greet parents in a cheerful manner.
- Sit with parents in the same type of chair.
- Listen carefully and never interrupt parents when they are expressing concerns.
- Focus on the future success of their child.
- Never discuss other people's children.

There are times when communication with parents is less than positive. Socioeconomic, linguistic, and ethnic diversity can create barriers to effective communication. You need to remember that the past educational experiences of the parents might influence the way they perceive and interact in the present. You can increase the comfort level of parents by creating opportunities for them that lead to successful experiences. Some ways teachers can incorporate parents into the learning environment are by asking them to share cultural traditions during a multicultural fair, assist with a field trip, or speak on career day.

Occasionally, parents must be summoned to address destructive or distracting student behaviors. These conferences should occur after the student has received a warning, met with the teacher or experienced other methods in an established chain of consequences. By going through the established chain of consequences, teachers demonstrate that they have given students the opportunity to correct their behavior.

It is advisable in most circumstances for the student to participate in the conference concerning their behavior for four reasons:

- A clearer picture develops of the events that contributed to the meeting.
- There is less of an opportunity for confusion to occur concerning future expectations.
- Students can take an active role in solving a problem that they initiated.
- Students will witness collaborative and cooperative modeling.

Conferences dealing with behavior provide the greatest opportunity to spread good will and model problem-solving strategies. You have the potential to positively influence the future of your students by helping them understand the relationship between particular behaviors and their consequences. By taking an active interest in the social well being of students, teachers demonstrate their professionalism and compassion to parents.

CHAPTER 12

PRACTICE TEST QUESTIONS

Read the following directions before beginning the practice questions.

- Read the entire guide as indicated in the introduction, highlighting unfamiliar concepts on the first reading and underlining concepts and facts with a pen or pencil on the second reading that are still not part of your knowledge repertoire.

- Sit at a desk or table and try not to leave until you have completed the entire practice exam. The more this exercise resembles an exam situation, the more accurately you will be able to gauge your future success.

- Give yourself two hours to complete the practice questions. If you find you did not have nearly enough time to finish, it is an indication that you will need to be more aware of your time when you take the actual *Principles of Learning and Teaching* Praxis exam.

- Do not skip questions. Instead, make an educated guess, then circle or answer the item number and proceed to the next question. This technique will save you time. If you have time remaining, return to any circled items to reread them. Remember, statistically your first answer is likely to be the right answer. It is always a good idea to recheck your answers when you have time remaining.

- Do not cheat! You cannot cheat on the actual test.

- When the two hours have passed or after you have completed and checked all of the questions, compare your answers to the *Answer Key*.

- The *Answer Key* for the multiple-choice questions lists the answers and the corresponding chapter for each question. Suggested responses for the case histories are provided in the recommended format. Read and review all of the questions you found difficult or answered incorrectly to understand terms and concepts.

Good luck!

Read the following and answer the three short-answer questions.

Leslie Hagan had been teaching third grade for four years before she had her first challenging ADHD inclusion student, Brett McCabe. "Frankly, I am not really sure that Brett is the whole problem." Leslie confided in her mentor, Linda Shaffer, from her first year induction program. "The parents are as much of a challenge as Brett. I try to avoid them at all costs. I have been trying to follow his IEP as directed, but frankly, there are a few requirements that just don't work in my classroom."

"What in particular are you bothered by?"

"Well whoever made the IEP must not know what goes on in a regular classroom. They want me to create routines for Brett, but I have 23 other children in the room. Why should Brett's needs come before the other children's? Also, the parents have requested that Brett be in an inclusive setting for most of the day. I think he would be better served by being in a self-contained classroom all day. The other students are tired of his disruptions and they are starting to avoid him. Frankly, I am tired of Brett too."

"Leslie, have you spoken to his special education teacher about your problems?"

"No, I'm afraid that he'll think I am unable to handle Brett, and I don't want the administration thinking that I am a whiner."

"What have you tried? I know Mrs. Miller, his second grade teacher, did pretty well with him."

"I let Brett do some of the running back and forth when I need to send things to the office, and I also allow him to pass out papers. But, frequently, he starts to horse around with another student and I have to take his morning recess away. The afternoon then is a total nightmare. He ends up being totally uncooperative and, to add insult to injury, his parents called me after school yesterday and asked why I have taken his recess away when the IEP specifies he is always to have recess. Linda, how am I supposed to discipline Brett if the parents keep coming to his rescue?"

Five minutes after Leslie spoke with her mentor she received another telephone call from Mrs. McCabe. It seems that Brett has been complaining of stomachaches in the morning and doesn't want to come to school. Leslie shared with Mrs. McCabe that Brett has made himself a target for the other children by being disruptive in the classroom and maybe that's why he's unhappy.

1. What comments regarding the IEP process support the fact that Leslie does not understand the laws regarding special education?
2. Why might Brett not want to attend school?
3. What should Leslie do to improve the situation?

SECOND CASE HISTORY

Read the following and answer the three short-answer questions.

Big River Middle School lies five miles from the Mexican border in a small town in Arizona. In order to provide the mostly low-income children in the area with the best physical plant and technology, the state assembled a task force to design and fund the new school. When Big River opened its doors in 2005, the State Board of Education hailed the facility as model to which all middle schools in Arizona should aspire.

Big River's initial enrollment topped 900 and included students from the three surrounding elementary schools: a nearby reservation school, a school of predominately immigrant children, and children from the nearby military base school. All these students came together for the first time in Big River's sixth grade. The inaugural school year began smoothly enough. The 112 parents who came to the open house during the first month were pleasantly surprised by the grandeur of the facility. Most of the newly hired teachers, however, were upset with the low parent turnout.

This wasn't the only aspect bothering the teachers. Last week twelve fights broke out on the playground, all of them between sixth graders, each of whom received two weeks of in-school suspension under the school's zero tolerance policy. Three of the students were from Susan Gregory's sixth grade class. When she tried to contact the students' parents for a meeting, two of the homes did not have telephones and the other child's parents did not speak English.

Another concern erupted when there was talk in the teachers' lounge that the State intended to move the date for achievement tests to the fall instead of the spring. Helen Palmer, a veteran teacher, expressed her concern. "Our students are already in the lowest quartile. How will prepare them without adequate time?"

Meanwhile, as the days passed, the students in Mrs. Gregory's classroom became increasingly segregated. The comment, "You should go back to Mexico where you belong!" earned Tommy Locke a detention. When Susan overheard a group of girls laughing about the clothes a Native American child wore, she immediately took away their recess for a week. It seemed as though things were escalating instead of coming under control. Something had to be done or it wouldn't matter that Big River Middle School was the State's model facility.

1. Big River Middle School has been provided with all of the material aspects a school might need to be successful. What facets were not considered?
2. How can the features that were not considered impact students' success?
3. What techniques could Susan Gregory use to encourage the acceptance of diversity among her classroom of sixth graders?

Read the following multiple-choice questions and select the best answer.

1. Which practice is not associated with Piagetian Theory?
   A. Identifying children with developmental delays
   B. Aligning state-mandated standards
   C. Selecting appropriate activities
   D. Designing appropriate activities

2. The Individuals with Disabilities Education Act (IDEA) mandates that educational rights are to be granted to all people in what age category?
   A. Birth to age twenty-one
   B. Three years old to age twenty-one
   C. Six years old to age eighteen
   D. Six years old to age twenty-one

3. According to Howard Gardner, a student who exhibits talents in perceiving visual images and imagined representations possesses which of the multiple intelligences?
   A. Bodily-kinesthetic intelligence
   B. Logical-mathematical intelligence
   C. Naturalist intelligence
   D. Spatial intelligence

4. Which is not one of the typical capabilities of a second grade child?
   A. Performing mental operations with the use of concrete objects
   B. Classification of items
   C. Conservation
   D. Hypothetical thinking

5. Teachers assess students' prior knowledge for all but which one of the following reasons?
   A. Identifying misconceptions
   B. Assess working memory
   C. Ascertaining interests
   D. Determining current levels of understanding

6. Maslow's Hierarchy of Needs suggests which scenario would most likely impair a student's ability to concentrate on intellectual pursuits?
   A. An undeveloped aesthetic appreciation
   B. A lack of interest in self-actualization
   C. Alienation from peers
   D. An unexpected outcome on one test

7. A third grade student who is punished for not meeting expectations will most likely suffer from which one of the following?
   A. Role-confusion
   B. Guilt
   C. Inferiority
   D. Shame

8. A foreign-language teacher pairs a fluent speaker with a less fluent speaker to practice a skit. Will this practice be successful or unsuccessful?
   A. Successful, the fluent speaker can provide support for the less fluent speaker
   B. Successful, the level of understanding has little to do with peer collaboration
   C. Unsuccessful, students learn language best through direct instruction
   D. Unsuccessful, the more fluent student gains little from the experience

9. All but which one of the following are effective ways to retain *fact-based* information?
   A. Rehearsal
   B. Meaningful learning
   C. Mnemonics
   D. Demonstration

10. Tracking, or ability grouping, is acceptable in which one of the following situations?
    A. Interests or vocational aspirations
    B. Intelligence or interests
    C. Ethnicity or vocational aspirations
    D. Tracking is never acceptable

11. Identify the element not necessary an Individualized Education Program (IEP).
    A. Present level of performance
    B. Strengths and needs to determine goals and objectives
    C. Instructional strategies and support services
    D. An explanation of the most restricted environment

12. A teacher who is designing a student-centered lesson would incorporate activities based upon which learning theory?
    A. Behaviorism
    B. Constructivism
    C. Developmental theory
    D. The zone of proximal development

Read the following and answer the three short-answer questions.

"Hey, Rich!" John Hayes walked into Mr. Evans 10th grade English class acting like he owned the place. As he circulated around the room visiting with his friends, Christopher Evans waited at the front of the room to take roll.

"John, you can sit down now or leave the room."

"Ah, Mr. Evans, you know you can't make me!" He grinned and finally sat in a seat in the back row.

Students in the class giggled and Mr. Evans began to call roll. "Sarah, is Sarah here?"

"She's in the bathroom."

"Rodrigo?" Christopher looked around the room.

"Lockup! He's in lockup!" A howl of laughter came from the class.

This was Christopher's first year teaching and now he understood why someone who had paid over $100,000 for his education would quit after his first year in the classroom. It was barely the third month and he was exhausted. He didn't understand how anybody could manage these students year after year.

Christopher had asked for help from other teachers but the suggestions seemed to get him in more trouble. "How about trying cooperative learning instead of always using direct instruction?" Kendra Morrison suggested. Cooperative learning was a total failure for Christopher. Students talked the whole period instead of working. Girls applied make-up in one group. In another group, all of the calculus students worked on their math homework. When Christopher approached them and asked what they thought they were doing, the students didn't even try to make an excuse.

Before class ended Christopher announced, "You all may think this class is just fun and games, but you have an exam coming up in three weeks, and right now I don't think anyone will pass it!"

"An exam?"

"On what?"

Mr. Evan's students' stunned expressions made him realize they were finally going to take him seriously.

1. What beginning classroom routines or organizational techniques should Christopher employ to improve the learning environment?
2. What advice would you give Mr. Evans regarding successful cooperative learning activities?
3. How might this teacher modify his method of assessment to increase classroom cooperation?

FOURTH CASE HISTORY

Read the following and answer the three short-answer questions.

All five members of the Student Assistance Team of Second Ward Elementary School looked up despondently after they read the case history of their next student, first grader Crystal Dutton. The surname was familiar to all of them. The Dutton family was known to have drifted in and out of homelessness for the last decade. All of the five older Dutton children had needed assistance from the team in some way.

"I wish I could say that there was hope, but if Crystal's brothers are an indication of our success rate with this family, it doesn't look positive."

"I think this might be the Dutton's last child. Let's see if we can make this count. I understand that Crystal functions at a normal cognitive level for her age." Joe Raad, the school counselor, smiled as if to indicate that the others should see this as a challenge to succeed.

"I have her for reading and she doesn't even know her letters. That could just be an indication of a lack of exposure. She is also painfully shy. At first, I thought she couldn't talk. I agree, Joe. I think we now have the resources and backing to make a difference." Vivian Goldstein seemed to be taking up the challenge. Her statement resulted in a flurry of planning by Joe Raad.

"Vivian, you and Crystal's other teachers should develop an individualized instruction plan for her. I will work with family services and the school nurse to make sure her other needs are met."

Two weeks later the team reconvened. "Vivian, tell us the academic plan for Crystal Dutton."

"Several issues came to mind when we discussed this child. We knew that we had to create some consistency at school. We also decided that by using peer scaffolding, we could maximize the amount of academic attention this little one will receive."

"Oh, I really like the peer idea." Joe interjected, "It dovetails nicely with what we were thinking about socially. I don't want that little girl to be a pariah. Let me share some suggestions from the nurse."

As the meeting continued, the formerly gloomy faces were marked by enthusiasm. It became clear that the Second Ward Student Assistance Team was determined to make a difference.

1. Are there human needs that might keep Crystal Dutton from being motivated to learn? Explain your answer.
2. What can teachers do to create a classroom that is conducive to learning for Crystal Dutton?
3. Explain what Vivian Goldstein meant when she said, "We also decided that by using peer scaffolding, we can maximize the amount of attention this little one will receive academically." Is this a sound educational idea?

Read the following multiple-choice questions and select the best answer.

1. Typical fifth-grade students would comply with school and classroom rules based upon what level of moral reasoning?
   A. Fear of being caught
   B. Adherence to rules is important
   C. Social contract
   D. Universal ethical principle

2. Performance-based assessment, or authentic assessment, is best characterized as which one of the following?
   A. A method to determine prior knowledge and establish readiness
   B. A way to emphasize student active responses that result in a product or event
   C. An evaluation where students must interact with the information by interpretation
   D. A method to determine the core knowledge a student has attained

3. Metacognition pertains to all but which one of the following answers?
   A. Students' extenuation in use of words, as in overgeneralization
   B. Students' knowledge of their own cognitive processes
   C. Students' awareness of their limitations
   D. Students' determination of personally effective study strategies

4. Teachers should accommodate individual learning styles of students for which one of the following reasons?
   A. Most school districts mandate such practices
   B. It increases student motivation
   C. Students advance incrementally
   D. It decreases time on-task

5. If a ninth grade teacher designs problem solving activities that are ill-defined, will the transfer of learning likely be successful or unsuccessful?
   A. Successful, because students like those types of problems
   B. Successful, because most problems outside of school are ill-defined
   C. Unsuccessful, because relevant information may be missing
   D. Unsuccessful, because goals may be unclear

6. Classroom environments should be structured to facilitate which of the following?
   A. Teacher control
   B. Student access
   C. Learning
   D. Student control

7. How are norm-reference scores accomplished?
   A. By having set criteria on which to base the test
   B. By comparing the performance of students
   C. By projecting expected performance on a test
   D. By determining what has and has not been learned

8. Which answer is not one of the benefits students receive when their parents are involved with their education?

    A. Increased attendance
    B. Improved attitudes toward school
    C. Increased academic achievement
    D. Increased dependence

9. Integrating the curriculum is beneficial for all but which one of the following reasons.

    A. It maintains the complexity of the actual environment
    B. Students use language from several disciplines to examine problems
    C. Methodology from various subject matter is utilized
    D. It primarily is skill-based and literal to reduce students' misconceptions

10. Which type of modeling would be most beneficial for a student struggling with an unfamiliar or difficult task?

    A. Teacher modeling
    B. Peer modeling
    C. Cultural modeling
    D. Parent modeling

11. Which of the following is not an acceptable modification for special education students?

    A. Adjusting the size of assignments
    B. Varying the time allotment for an assignment
    C. Decreasing the level of difficulty
    D. Assigning homework to introduce concepts

12. Teachers should base rules for the classroom on which one of the following factors?

    A. The rules children's parents have in their home
    B. The developmental stage of the children
    C. What rules the children in the classroom determine as a group
    D. What has traditionally been prescribed in schools

ANSWER KEY FOR THE MULITPLE-CHOICE QUESTIONS

Question	Correct Response	Chapter Reference
1	B	2. The Cognitive Development of Students
2	A	9. Special Education
3	D	11. Teacher Professionalism
4	D	2. The Cognitive Development of Students
5	B	5. Cognition and Knowledge Construction
6	C	8. Motivation
7	C	3. The Psychosocial Development of Students
8	A	2. The Cognitive Development of Students
9	D	5. Cognition and Knowledge Construction
10	A	4. Student Diversity
11	D	9. Special Education
12	B	7. Instructional Design
1	B	3. The Psychosocial Development of Students
2	B	10. Student Assessment
3	A	2. The Cognitive Development of Students
4	B	4. Student Diversity
5	B	7. Instructional Design
6	C	6. Creating an Environment for Student Learning
7	B	10. Student Assessment
8	D	11. Teacher Professionalism
9	D	5. Cognition and Knowledge Construction
10	B	8. Motivation
11	D	9. Special Education
12	B	6. Creating an Environment for Student Learning

1. It is clear that Leslie Hagan does not understand the laws and accepted practices associated with special education for the following reasons:
   - The IEP is a legal document that must be followed.
   - Participants in the IEP process include a regular classroom teacher so that procedures and suggestions are feasible in the regular classroom.
   - IDEA mandates that Brett be in the least restrictive environment. Because he had a successful second grade year, he is probably capable of being in the regular classroom.
   - Because parents are part of the IEP process, Leslie should try to work with them to create a more successful setting and learning experience for Brett.
   - Leslie should work with Brett's special education teacher to attain a better understanding of his exceptionality.

2. Brett might not want to attend school for the following reasons:
   - The other children are avoiding him.
   - He might sense that his teacher does not like him.
   - He has had his morning recess taken away.
   - Brett is given a task, passing out papers, that frequently results in punishment.

3. Leslie Hagan should do the following to improve Brett's situation:
   - Teachers act as models for their students. If students perceive that Ms. Hagan does not like Brett, they will likely follow suit. Leslie should model behaviors that reflect a respect and acceptance of all children.
   - Leslie needs to find the talents Brett processes and use those talents to establish his worth in the classroom with the other children.
   - Leslie should work with the special education teacher, the McCabes, and Brett to establish consequences that deter his bad behavior and are consistent with his IEP.
   - Leslie should establish routines in her classroom not only for Brett but for the other children as well. Routines increase time

on task and help to create a predictable and safe environment for all students.

SUGGESTED REPONSES FOR THE SECOND CASE HISTORY

1. Two major aspects were not managed or considered by the administration and teaching faculty at Big River Middle School. The School has a diverse group of children coming together for the first time. The school neglected to consider that this new union of students might need to be managed in some way. The second important factor that the school did not consider was their large number of low-income students.

2. Diversity and poverty can impact the education process in several ways:
    *   Students with limited English skills are at high risk for dropping out of school.
    *   Instructional adaptations might be necessary for ESL students to be academically successful.
    *   Multicultural education should be employed to successfully integrate the various diverse groups into their new school environment and create a climate of acceptance.
    *   Students from low-income households are more likely to drop out of school or become pregnant out of wedlock, and are more prone to health risks.

3. Susan Gregory could use the following techniques to facilitate an environment of acceptance:
    *   She can utilize culturally diverse cooperative learning groups so that students have a unified purpose and can become familiar with each other's cultures and perspectives.
    *   She should incorporate the perspectives and achievements of culturally diverse individuals into the curriculum to establish the worth of all cultures.
    *   She can draw upon students' unique experiences to motivate individual students and establish their value in the classroom.
    *   Susan should become familiar with the various cultures represented in her classroom to increase her understanding and appreciation for their diversity.

- Susan can encourage the families or guardians of her students to become involved in the education of their children by attending school functions and participating in classroom activities.

SUGGESTED REPONSES FOR THE THIRD CASE HISTORY

1. Christopher Evans should do the following to improve the behavior of his students:
   - He should have a seating chart.
   - He should have an assignment on the board for students to do when they arrive in class.
   - He should take roll silently while students do their beginning assignment.
   - He should establish consequences for noncompliance and consistently apply them.

2. Mr. Evans should do the following when utilizing cooperative learning groups:
   - He should create groups of mixed ability.
   - He should place students in groups based upon their capacity to work together.
   - He should establish common group goals with clear guidelines for outcomes and behavior.
   - He should create individual tasks for group members to encourage group interdependence.
   - He should establish time limits.
   - He should communicate to students that their final assessment will encompass both their individual performance and the group's performance

3. Mr. Evans should make the following modifications:
   - Students should be assessed on a regular basis using both formative and summative methods.
   - Assessment on a regular basis will motivate students to apply themselves daily and inform them of their progress.
   - Mr. Evans should make a habit of posting the learning objectives daily.

- Students should be aware of what they are responsible for learning and how those objectives relate to assessment.

Suggested Reponses for the Fourth Case History

1. Yes, there are needs that can interfere with the desire to learn. Because Crystal Dutton has been homeless she might have the following deficiency needs, according to Maslow:
   - She might lack the basic physiological needs such as food and rest.
   - Because of parental stress due to homelessness and tentative living conditions, she may not always be safe.
   - She may not be accepted by other students since she is living in poverty. This could result in a feeling of not belonging.
   - If she is unable to achieve or be accepted by her peers she might suffer from low self-esteem.

2. Crystal's teachers can do several things to create an environment conducive to learning:
   - Because of Crystal's haphazard living conditions, her teachers should try to make the school environment as predictable as possible so she has a feeling of safety. This would include having consistent rules and classroom routines.
   - Crystal's teachers should also make sure her personal needs are met. Clothing, food, and health care needs can all be met through most public school systems and their associated social service agencies.
   - Crystal might also need assistance from her teachers in developing friendships. If Crystal's teachers encourage friendships through cooperative learning activities and highlight the talents of all students in the classroom, hopefully an environment of acceptance will result.
   - Crystal's academic progress should be monitored often through formative assessment. The team might also need to consider special education screening for Crystal to ensure that she obtains all the assistance she is entitled to receive.

3. Vivian Goldstein probably was referring to using other children to assist with Crystal's learning. Peer scaffolding means using

students to explain concepts and provide support for other students. Cooperative learning and peer tutoring are just two ways that peer scaffolding is used in the classroom. This is a sound educational idea for the following reasons:

- Having similar others explain ideas to students gives them the hope that they too are capable of understanding.
- Peer tutors explaining ideas must use metacognitive skills, which improves their retention of material.
- Activities such as cooperative learning and peer tutoring help to create an environment of understanding and acceptance if properly monitored.

REFERENCES

Banks, J. A., & Banks, C. A. M. (1997). *Multicultural education: Issues and perspectives* (3rd ed.).Boston, MA: Allyn & Bacon.

Driscoll, M. P., McCown, R. R., Roop, P. G., Griffin, M. M., & Quinn, G. P. (1996). *Educational psychology: A learning-centered approach to classroom practice.* Boston, MA: Allyn & Bacon.

Eggen, P., & Kauchak, D. (1999). *Educational psychology: Windows on classrooms.* Upper Saddle River, NJ: Merrill/Prentice Hall.

Henniger, M. L. (2004). *The teaching experience: An introduction to reflective practice.* Upper Saddle River, NJ: Merrill/Prentice Hall.

Heward, W. L. (2000). *Exceptional children: An introduction to special education.* Upper Saddle River, NJ: Merrill/Prentice Hall.

Jones, V. F., & Jones, L. S. (2001). *Comprehensive classroom management.* Boston, MA: Allyn & Bacon.

Lefrancois, G. R. (1999). *Psychology for teaching.* Ontario, Canada: Wadsworth.

Levin, J., & Nolan, J. F. (2000). *Principles of classroom management.* Boston, MA: Allyn & Bacon.

No Child Left Behind Act. (2002). Retrieved September 26, 2002, from http://www.ed.gov/legislation/ESEA02/pgl.html#sec101

Ormrod, J. E. (2006). *Educational psychology: Developing learners* (5th edition), Upper Saddle River, NJ: Merrill/Prentice Hall.

Postman, R. D. (1999). *How to prepare for the Praxis.* Hauppauge, NY: Barron's Educational Series, Inc.

Santrock, J. W. (2001). *Educational psychology.* New York, NY: McGraw-Hill.

Shorall, C. (2000). *Changing relationships in education.* Hamden, Connecticut: International Society for Exploring Teaching Alternatives.

Wong, H. K. & Wong, R. T. (1998). *The first days of school.* Mountain View, CA: Harry K.Wong Publications, Inc.